Eat To Your Heart's Content

without the guilt

Jayne Meade

Eat To Your Heart's Content

First hardback edition published in the United Kingdom in 2014

Text and recipes copyright © Jayne Meade 2014
Photography copyright © Jayne Meade 2014

Design and layout copyright © Luke Guppy 2014
www.guppycreative.com

For additional copies of this book please email enquiries@skinnygrub.co.uk

Further information: Website: www.skinnygrub.co.uk

The moral rights of the author has been asserted.

ISBN 978-0-9929611-0-7

A catalogue record for this book is available from the British Library.

Printed in Great Britain by Tyson Press.
London, W1D 2EU | Chester, CH4 9QR

Dedicated to the next generation.

What we teach our children not only teaches our children but also their children and so on to the end of generations.

Anon

About the Author

As well as being a wife and mother of three, Jayne Meade's passion is, and always has been, food.

Juggling kids, life and everything, Jayne managed to find time, during those early blissful years of marriage, to pursue her passion for food and enrolled in a three year City and Guilds professional cookery course and life has not been the same since – mostly in a good way she thinks.

After passing the City and Guilds course with distinction, she taught basic and professional cookery at a private school, which fitted in nicely with family life. She later entered the world of cut-throat freelance catering, which, taught her that there must be a better way to make a living. A by-product however, was that this gave her the opportunity to develop her creative side, experimenting with recipes, flavours and ingredients. She later went on to study at the world famous Le Cordon Bleu Institute in London on their patisserie programme.

Jayne's other claim to fame is that she has considerable experience at over indulging and has tried every diet going in a quick fix attempt to shed unwanted pounds and along with the best of them, failed miserably. However, she eventually discovered a nationwide slimming group, which opened the door to a whole new concept of controlled eating. Eventually, enthralled by this concept, Jayne became a consultant with the group to spread the word.

As her creative cooking side started to gain momentum, which included her knowledge of slimming and healthy eating, she eventually decided to develop a range of recipes of normal, everyday food made with healthy ingredients, which she hopes will help people enjoy a healthier life style.

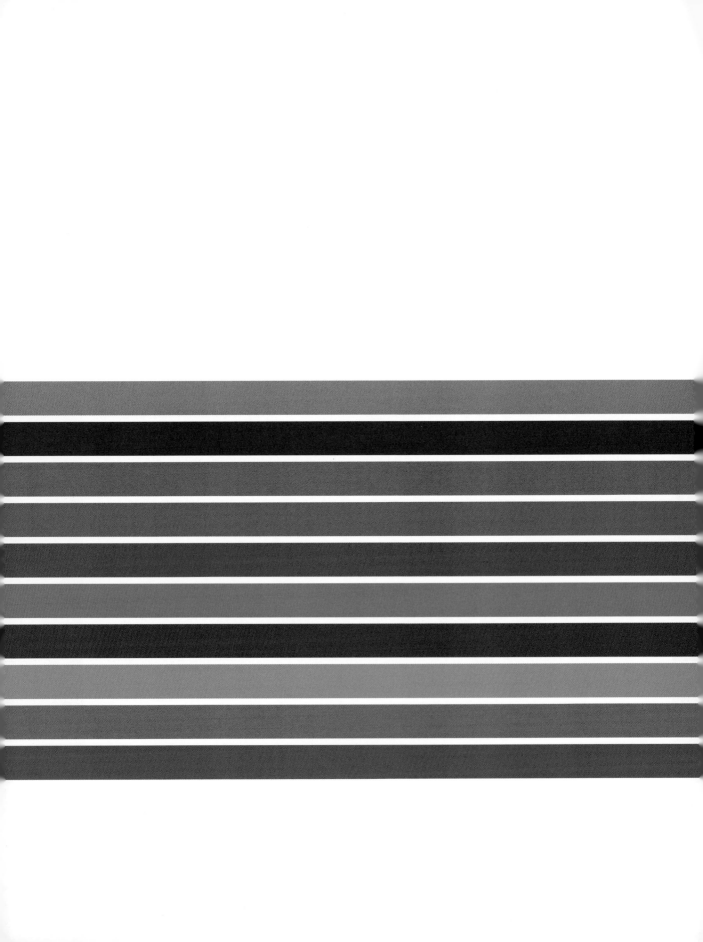

Contents

Acknowledgements

I would like to take this opportunity (at the risk of repeating myself as I am often prone to do and which I am continuously teased about by my nearest and dearest) to acknowledge the support and encouragement I have received over the years.

My eternal gratitude to my amazing husband Carl, for your tireless patience and endless enthusiasm in almost everything I have set my mind upon. Your support and love is unconditional. This book would not have been possible if it hadn't been for you.

To my wonderful children, Nicola, Kelly and Lewis, thank you for all your support, love, encouragement and constructive criticism - I think that's what it was. You all share so many positive qualities and yet are so unique in many ways. Nicola, thank you for tirelessly editing my initial drafts and for bringing so many creative ideas and suggestions forward. Your forthright and honest approach has been so important in the making of this book. I am sure that your remarkable business acumen along with your professionalism will turn your own business venture, Pretty Parcels Cakery, into a resounding success. Kelly, your uncompromising principles, strength and determination to succeed are an inspiration to us all. You have been a great sounding board for ideas and suggestions and I have always appreciated your thought provoking feedback. Lewis, you have shown amazing talent in the world of media and entertainment and hopefully (hint, hint) my YouTube "How to make a Healthy New York Cheesecake" video should soon be followed by a selection from this book. If I can harness all of your combined energies and qualities my ambition for SkinnyGrub will be more than just a dream. You three are my greatest achievement. I love you all.

A huge thank you to my son-in-law Luke, your hard work, patience and amazing imagination has transformed my ideas onto paper making my book exactly as I had imagined. You really are brilliant and fantastic at what you do! I love you too.
To Jayne Schmidt, for your continued patience, encouragement and support throughout my slimming years – again you're great at what you do. And to all my fellow slimming buddies, especially Chris, thank you all for your continued support and encouragement, especially during our taster evenings which provided so much encouraging feedback that spurred me on to write this book.

Thank you all.

Introduction

'EAT To Your Hearts Content' is a down to earth recipe book of normal everyday food but using healthier ingredients, which as the title suggests is the essence of this book.

The inspiration behind this book comes from my own life experiences of food and family and the ever-deteriorating state of the nation's health. Consider the continuous media coverage of the obesity epidemic and the link of over indulgence to so many related ailments such as diabetes, heart disease, dementia to name but a few. The old adage 'you are what you eat' has never rung so true. However, changing eating habits of a lifetime are easier said than done, which is why diets constantly fail.

This conundrum forms the focus of this book – why not simply adapt the recipes of the dishes that we all enjoy and change how the food is prepared. Contained in this book are over 100 every day dishes that have been creatively and subtly transformed into healthier equivalents, virtually indistinguishable from the original.

Although this is not a diet book, it recognises the positive impact of healthy eating on an individual's weight. It includes tried and tested healthy recipes with simple to follow instructions that can be eaten by the family unit – one meal for all.

Following these recipes will be a major step in changing eating habits for a lifetime and begs the question why other cookbooks don't follow this approach – full of flavour but low in fat, salt and sugar. The recipes are exciting, delicious and brimming with imagination and destroys the myth that eating healthy and losing weight need to be boring.

Food is my livelihood and my passion. It's also my nemesis, which makes an interesting twist to my life and the motivation behind this book.

One of the major influences in my life and probably the step that changed my attitude towards food was when I became a mother. From day one you suddenly have total responsibility for the wellbeing of the most precious thing in your life and how your child develops from this point forward is down to you, which of course includes their eating habits.

Your little bundles of joy have no way of knowing what's good or bad to eat, they take their lead from you and gradually over time develop their own habits based upon what you teach them. At times, poisoning the little buggers can be a temptation, but mum (or dad) is the one person who has the power to influence their eating habits for life and by implication their short and long-term health and well being. Don't blame society or the fast food restaurants or the food manufacturers. They didn't make you have kids and they won't be there to sort out their health problems in the future. How they grow up and develop is down to you. Unfortunately over time as they grow you become the last person they listen to but, by that time, your work should be done – for good or bad you'll have set the tone for their future.

I guess that this is when I really started to experiment with more healthy ingredients in recipes whilst trying to retain the flavours and visual presentation that would appeal to my family.

Eating is also a great social event creating the opportunity for family and friends to assemble and share experiences. On such occasions food needs to be interesting and enjoyable. Following the recipes in this book will fulfill these expectations whilst providing that extra dimension of healthy eating with or without the knowledge of your guests. I frequently serve the recipes from this book when we have a gathering but keep quiet about the healthy ingredients as in reality no one can tell the difference.

Anyone following a structured weight control plan wanting to add a degree of normality back into their lives can do so by using the recipes from this book. The recipes can be an excellent addition to many of the well-known diet plans out there.

There are over 100 recipes for everyday meals with easy to follow instructions as well as photographs, taken by me at the time each recipe was prepared, depicting what the finished dish should look like. No photographic trickery or food imitation substitutes have been used - what you see is what you get!

The recipes and instructions are intended to be easy to follow, however I do realise there is a wide range of cooking experience out there and of course not everyone is a trained chef. If your ability is anything like my husbands, bless him, you may need a few tips and pointers, well maybe a lot more than a few. Visit my website www.skinnygrub.co.uk, which contains lots of useful information as well as a Q&A forum.

Enjoy your cooking and remember, like all things in life, the more practise you get, the easier it becomes and your confidence will grow. Don't forget to be creative and develop your own variations to these recipes and let me know via the website any ideas you come up with.

Good luck and enjoy.

Jayne x.

A Note About the Ingredients

BREAD
Wholemeal bread is my preferred choice as it contains the wholegrain and subsequently has its fibre intact. Brown bread, on the other hand, is white flour dyed with caramel so devoid of any fibre. Again select whichever choice you prefer.

COOKING SPRAY
Low calorie cooking spray, containing only 1 calorie per spray, is used extensively throughout the book. It produces excellent results when frying onions, mushrooms, chips, roast potatoes, a cooked breakfast and even for greasing tins. Cooking with oil, on the other hand, adds unwanted calories to meals so give the low calorie version a try and you might be converted. At the time of writing this book low calorie cooking sprays are available in five flavours; sunflower, extra virgin olive oil, butter, garlic and stir-fry.

EGGS
All recipes in this book are prepared using large free-range eggs but use whatever size and type you prefer. Since the salmonella scare all eggs should have the Lion quality mark printed on them to show that the hens have been vaccinated against salmonella. However, the advice when cooking for the elderly, young, pregnant or those with weakened immune systems or debilitating illness is to avoid raw eggs. (www.lioneggs. co.uk for more information). All Lion quality eggs are date stamped for freshness giving a best before date.

FRUIT AND VEGETABLES
I prefer to leave the skin on fruit and vegetables as it contains valuable fibre and nutrients but peel if you wish. Make sure you scrub them well before using.

HERBS AND SPICES
Dried herbs and spices are absent of any oil unlike the paste varieties so use these wherever possible.

MEAT AND POULTRY
Always select lean meat and remove any visible fat before cooking. Unfortunately the saturated fat on meat and poultry contains flavour so by removing this you are removing a lot of the flavour. To counteract this you can re-introduce the flavour back in the form of herbs, spices and flavourings, the upside being flavour without the calories!

If preparing a casserole and time allows, prepare the dish the night before and refrigerate overnight. Before reheating the next day, any fat that has risen to the surface can easily be skimmed off with a spoon.

Remove the skin from all poultry and the rind and fat from bacon before cooking as these contain vast amounts of saturated fat. Unfortunately, if not removed before cooking, temptation may get the better of you once cooked – believe me I know what I am talking about!

Always select the extra lean varieties of mince to reduce the amount of saturated fat.

MEAT ALTERNATIVES
QUORN is a meat free, extremely versatile product, suitable for vegetarians. However, the inclusion of egg white and milk proteins makes it unsuitable for vegans. It's low in fat and high in protein and fibre. It can be purchased in ready-made meals, or the plain versions are available in the form of mince and chunks. The mince variety has 75% less fat than lean beef mince so is worth considering. If trying it out on family or friends for the first time don't divulge this, as they will never know the difference. Further information about quorn can be found at www.quorn.co.uk.

SOYA meat free products are available as mince or chunks and can be substituted for meat or Quorn, just follow packet instructions.

MILK
There are many types and varieties of milk available including cow's, sheep, goat, soya, oat, rice, almond, hazelnut and a light version of coconut milk (not to be confused with the tinned coconut milk variety). Most are found either in fresh or ambient form, with the fat content ranging from 0.1% to 4%+. There are many options to choose from to reduce the fat content in cooking without you really noticing the difference.

QUARK
Quark is a virtually fat free soft cheese found in the chiller cabinet, alongside the cheeses, in supermarkets. Its bland taste requires the addition of herbs, spices or other ingredients to make it more palatable. When cooking with Quark extreme care is needed due to its lack of fat, as it'll split if used over a high heat - the addition of eggs will help to prevent this splitting. I use Quark mainly in cold dishes but substitute silken

tofu in hot dishes (see note on silken tofu).

RICE, PASTA, NOODLES

Dried rice, pasta and noodles are available in enormous varieties. Wholegrain varieties require a little more cooking but have more flavour than their white counterparts and provide extra fibre, which is always a good thing.

SUGAR FREE PRODUCTS AND SWEETENERS

There is a lot of available information about "artificial sweeteners" versus "natural sugar". Artificial sweeteners are available in supermarkets in the form of granules or in tablet form. You may be surprised to find that many of the prepared foods you buy contain them in one form or another. They are widely used in the food industry - check out the product labeling. Research the facts for yourselves and then decide what your own preference is. If you prefer not to use them then substitute with sugar in the recipes but beware of the accompanying calories.

At the time of writing this book I have become aware of a new sweetener that is available on UK supermarket shelves. It originates from a natural plant called Stevia and claims to be more than 200 times sweeter than sugar but without the calories. It's been used as a natural sweetener in South America and Asia for many years. Research the facts available on the internet to find out more about this product.

YOGHURT, FROMAGE FRAIS, SILKEN TOFU

Vast arrays of yoghurts fill the shelves of supermarkets making this a very competitive market and mind baffling to choose from. Select low fat or fat free versions to keep the fat content of your meal down. Greek 0% fat Total yoghurt tastes delicious and in my opinion has a more creamy and thicker consistency than other low fat/fat free yoghurts/fromage frais varieties. But be careful, not all low fat/fat free yoghurts/fromage frais are as innocent as you'd think as they contain added sugar, so read the labels and make your selection accordingly.

Care needs to be taken when cooking with low fat/fat free yoghurts/fromage frais because if cooked on a high heat they have a tendency to split (due to the absence of fat) resulting in the appearance of your dish being spoilt, although the taste will not be affected. To overcome this problem, add a beaten egg to it but don't allow it to boil. This will help to stabilise the consistency. My preferred choice however, when cooking, is to use silken tofu as it more stable than other low fat/fat free yoghurt/fromage frais.

It's available in a variety of consistencies from extra firm to soft. If making dips or sauces, I recommend you use the soft variety. It will need to be blended together to transform it from a semi-block to a lump-free semi-liquid that will have the consistency of lightly whipped cream. It can be found in ambient packets on the supermarket shelves or in specialist stores. It's a great product that can be used either hot or cold and I really recommend you give it a go.

STOCKS

Reserve any cooking liquid from vegetables, as this will produce a light stock. For a chicken stock, cover the carcass, from your Sunday roast, with water and throw in a few vegetables and herbs, simmer for about an hour and strain. Leave to cool and refrigerate overnight where any fat present will have risen to the surface and can be skimmed off the next day. For a more intense flavour boil the skimmed stock until reduced by half. Failing that use stock cubes that are readily available in a variety of flavours. For speed and taste I prefer using Stock Pots, again available in several flavours, as they taste less manufactured than stock cubes. One pot will produce 500ml of stock when dissolved in boiling water. They can be added directly into casseroles, sauces, pasta etc. where they will melt and enhance the flavour of your dish.

SALT

The recommended daily allowance of salt intake for adults is no more than 6g - that's around one level teaspoon, (children should eat less) so season sensibly. Also be aware that salt (sodium) can be found in prepared foods so regularly check the labels. For more information refer to www.nhs.uk.

SEAFOOD

Information on sustainable seafood can be obtained in the first instance from www.fishonline.org.

Conversion Tables

OVEN TEMPERATURES

Celcius	Fahrenheit	Gas
110C	225F	¼
130C	250F	½
140C	275F	1
150C	300F	2
170C	325F	3
180C	350F	4
190C	375F	5
200C	400F	6
220C	425F	7
230C	455F	8

SPOON MEASURES

Metric	Imperial
5ml	1 tsp
10ml	2 tsp
15ml	1 tbsp
30ml	2 tbsp
45ml	3 tbsp
60ml	4 tbsp
75ml	5 tbsp
90ml	6 tbsp

For fan assisted ovens reduce temperatures by 20C lower than stated in the recipe or according to your oven instruction booklet.

WEIGHT

Metric	Imperial
15g	½oz
25g	1oz
50g	2oz
75g	3oz
100g	3½oz
110g	4oz
150g	5oz
175g	6oz
200g	7oz
225g	8oz
250g	9oz
275g	10oz
300g	11oz
350g	12oz

Metric	Imperial
375g	13oz
400g	14oz
425g	15oz
450g	1lb
500g	1lb 2oz
550g	1lb 4oz
600g	1lb 6oz
700g	1lb 9oz
750g	1lb 10oz
800g	1lb 12oz
850g	1lb 14oz
900g	2lb
1kg	2lb 4oz

The metric conversions are approximate rather than precise in order to make cooking and weighing out simpler. The actual metric conversion of 1oz is 28g.

VOLUME

Metric	Imperial
30ml	1fl oz
60ml	2fl oz
90ml	3fl oz
100ml	3½fl oz
120ml	4fl oz
150ml	5fl oz/¼ pint
180ml	6fl oz
200ml	7fl oz
240ml	8fl oz
270ml	9fl oz
300ml	10fl oz/½ pint
360ml	12fl oz
400ml	14fl oz
450ml	16fl oz
500ml	18fl oz
600ml	20fl oz/1 pint
800ml	28fl oz
900ml	1½ pint
1 litre	34fl oz
1.25 litre	2 pints
1.5 litre	2½ pints

LINEAR

Metric	Imperial
2.5cm	1in
3cm	1¼in
4cm	1½in
5cm	2in
5.5cm	2¼in
6cm	2½in
7cm	2¾in
7.5cm	3in
8cm	3¼in
9cm	3½in
10cm	4in
11cm	4¼in

Metric	Imperial
12cm	4½in
13cm	5in
14cm	5½in
15cm	6in
16cm	6¼in
17cm	6½in
18cm	7in
19cm	7½in
20cm	8in
22cm	8½in
23cm	9in
24cm	9½in
25cm	10in

Breakfasts

Boiled Eggs with a difference

Boiled eggs are great for breakfast and will set you up for the morning ahead. If you don't want to accompany your eggs with the traditional 'soldiers', (not that there's anything wrong with them), you could try serving them with dunkable asparagus or crispy grilled bacon rashers. A strange combination you might think but I guarantee you'll be licking your fingers long after. I haven't listed any quantities for asparagus or bacon – that's down to you!

Serves 1

lean bacon, all visible fat removed

asparagus spears, stalk-end removed

low calorie cooking spray

2 eggs

salt and pepper

Grill or fry the bacon and asparagus in the low calorie cooking spray, turning regularly until the asparagus spears are tender and the bacon is crispy enough to be dunked.

Whilst these are cooking, place the eggs into a saucepan of cold water and bring to the boil. Boil for 3 minutes if you like your eggs soft and runny, or cook according to your preference. Then place them into eggcups, slice off their tops and serve with the crispy bacon and asparagus spears. Season to taste with a little salt and pepper.

Breakfast Congee

Now, I'm a morning person and always eat breakfast. If I don't I'll be starving by mid-morning. So if there ever is a breakfast I look forward to, it's this. Actually, to be absolutely honest, I'd prefer a lovely bowl of thick porridge drizzled with golden syrup and double cream, (now you're talking), but let's face it, it'll go straight on the thighs forever more to stay. Breakfast Congee however, is nearly as good, and I can eat it everyday without any guilt.

I never tire of this dish because it can be varied in so many ways. Change the fruit, eat hot or cold, drizzled with milk or fat free fruit yoghurt, sprinkle with cinnamon, or try the savoury version. You can make it in one batch, cool quickly and store for about three days in the refrigerator for those moments when you need breakfast to go. One very important point to note is that rice needs careful storing and reheating. It must be served very cold or very hot in order to kill any bacterial spores present. So carry it with an ice block if taking to work and store in the fridge until needed. Personally I can't wait that long!

Serves 4-6

BASIC CONGEE

300g Jasmine Thai rice or any other long grain rice

5 green cardamom pods cracked open (optional)

1 litre water

Place the rice in a medium saucepan with the cardamom pods (if using) and water. Bring to the boil, reduce the heat and simmer until the water has been absorbed, stirring regularly and quite robustly. The idea is to break down the rice so it gels together. Add more water if it starts to stick. It can take between 30-60 minutes until the correct consistency is reached. When cooked eat immediately or cool and refrigerate.

SWEET CONGEE

basic congee recipe

sweetener (to taste)

fat free yoghurt/skimmed milk

fruit of your choice

FOR THE SWEET CONGEE
Prepare the basic congee recipe and serve with sweetener, drizzle with milk or top with yoghurt and fruit.

SAVOURY CONGEE

basic congee recipe

For the dressing

2 tablespoons fish sauce

juice ½ lime

juice ½ orange

1cm ginger, peeled and finely grated

SUPER HEALTHY VERSION

basic congee recipe but substitute
white rice for brown rice

any toppings of your choice

FOR THE SAVOURY CONGEE

Prepare the basic congee recipe. Place the dressing ingredients in a clean jam jar, screw on the lid and shake. Drizzle over the hot congee and enjoy. It will certainly wake up those brain cells!

FOR THE SUPER HEALTHY VERSION

Now, for me a bowl of congee is simply divine and real comfort food. But if you want to appear virtuous, opt for this healthier version using brown rice. The difference between white and brown rice is that white rice has been processed and has the outer shell removed, losing a lot of the goodness in the process, whereas the brown version contains the shell along with all it's vitamins, minerals and fibre. It's goodness in a grain! I was pleasantly surprised after trying this recipe as it comes very close to the original one, plus you instantly feel a glowing halo hovering above your head with every mouthful. Try it, it might just surprise you!

To prepare, make the basic congee recipe but substitute the white rice with brown. It takes longer to cook, nearly an hour or more until you reach the right consistency, so allow a little extra time or make it the day before and chill in the refrigerator. You'll probably need to add more water during the cooking period to prevent it sticking. Remember to stir occasionally.

Again, serve either with the sweet or savoury toppings or have a go at inventing your own.

Jayne's Tips

This can double up as a really comforting snack. Don't tell the family how good it is otherwise there'll be nothing left!

Add chopped chilli and drizzle with a little sesame oil for variety.

Chopped spring onions cooked in low calorie cooking spray along with a little garlic and scattered on top also tastes yummy. If you don't have time, serve with raw chopped spring onions or pickled ginger.

My Full English

A full English breakfast tends to be avoided by many as it carries that unhealthy tag. Well not any more! This recipe balances the full English breakfast experience with the desire for healthy eating and should be a hit with the entire family.

Serves 4

4 large potatoes, scrubbed

low calorie cooking spray

4-8 tomatoes, halved (depending on your appetite)

4 large capped mushrooms or 500g button mushrooms

8 fat free/low fat sausages (or vegetarian alternative)

8 rashers lean back bacon

8 eggs

1 large can baked beans

Preheat the oven to 200C/Gas 6.

Microwave each potato for approximately 6 minutes. If you're pushed for time this can be done the day before, cooled and kept in the refrigerator until needed. When cool enough to handle, cut into large chunks and place onto a baking tray that has been sprayed with low calorie cooking spray along with the tomatoes, mushrooms and sausages. Spray again and bake until cooked through, about 20-25 minutes.

Fry the bacon and eggs in the spray and heat the baked beans until piping hot. Once everything is ready, dish-up and enjoy.

For the hungriest appetites serve with wholemeal toast.

Jayne's Tips

Why not make a Full English Breakfast Sandwich if you're really hungry. You might need a knife and fork to tackle it or just dive in with your fingers. Yum!

Use up any leftover potato wedges, boiled or roast potatoes in this recipe.

Quinoa Porridge

Not many people know about this wonderful grain. It's been around for at least 3,000 years and was used by the Incas who believed the grain to be sacred, referring to it as the 'mother of all grains'. It's a complete protein (unlike beans or peas) containing essential amino acids, good quantities of phosphorus, magnesium and iron and is also a good source of dietary fibre. It's high in calcium making it useful for the lactose intolerant and vegans.

When cooked Quinoa has a light and fluffy texture with a mild, slightly nutty flavour making it an alternative to couscous and rice. Well enough of the history lesson, let's make the dish.

**Makes 5 bowls
depending on appetite**

1 cup Quinoa

2 cups water

TO SERVE

fresh fruit

skimmed milk/fat free yoghurt

cinnamon

sweetener

Place the Quinoa and water into a medium sized saucepan and bring to the boil. Cover with a lid and simmer for 10 minutes until the water has been absorbed.

Remove from the heat and leave to stand for 5 minutes. Serve with fresh fruit, a drizzle of milk or a dollop of yoghurt. For a different flavour, try adding a touch of cinnamon or some sweetener.

Any remaining Quinoa can be covered and stored in the refrigerator until needed.

Jayne's Tips

Eat hot or cold for breakfast or use in place of couscous or rice for a super healthy salad.

It's better to rinse Quinoa before cooking, if it hasn't already been done, as this removes the saponins, its bitter coating.

Light as a cloud Pancakes

I love pancakes but find that one is never enough. Traditional pancakes are made with flour, sugar, butter, milk and eggs containing many calories and fat. This version is low in fat so can be eaten whenever you want without feeling guilty. They're light and fluffy and surprisingly filling and I like to serve them with sugar free maple syrup or my favourite is with fat free vanilla yoghurt and loads of fresh berries. A perfect start to a lazy weekend. Check out my other pancake recipe on p.28 for a healthy alternative to the traditional pancake.

Makes 12 small pancakes

120g very low fat cottage cheese

2 eggs, separated

1 teaspoon vanilla extract

2 tablespoons sweetener (to taste)

low calorie cooking spray

TO SERVE

fresh berries, fat free yoghurt or sugar free maple syrup

Firstly blitz the cottage cheese in a food processor until smooth, or rub through a sieve. Add the egg yolks, the vanilla extract and sweetener (if using) and mix well.

In a separate bowl whisk the egg whites until stiff. Carefully fold them into the cottage cheese mixture, a third at a time, taking care not to beat otherwise all the air will be knocked out and your pancakes will be heavy.

Heat a frying pan that's been sprayed with low calorie cooking spray over a medium heat and drop spoonfuls of the batter into the pan, cooking until golden brown. Flip over and cook for another 30 seconds. Keep warm and repeat this process with the remaining mixture. Serve with whatever toppings you fancy.

Jayne's Tips

Add grated orange zest or cinnamon, or fold in some fresh blueberries.

Make these for yourself when the family are tucking into their traditional pancakes, then you won't feel as if you're missing out - a key to losing weight.

Pancakes

Pancakes are so versatile and can feature for breakfast, lunch, dinner or dessert but the traditional version can be unhealthy. My version doesn't contain any sugar or butter like traditional recipes so you won't feel as guilty after eating them. If like me you have difficulty stopping at two pancakes, then check out the 'light as a cloud pancake recipe' see recipe on p.27.

Makes 8-10 depending on size of pan and thickness of batter

100g plain flour, sifted

pinch salt

2 eggs, beaten

200ml skimmed milk

75ml water

low calorie cooking spray

TO SERVE

lemon juice

sweetener

honey

fruit

low fat/fat free yoghurt

Make the batter by sieving the flour and salt into a large mixing bowl and make a well in the centre. In a separate bowl, whisk together the eggs, milk and water. Then pour this liquid into the well and using a whisk, gradually blend into the flour starting from the centre working outwards. Once incorporated, beat well until you have a smooth silky batter. This can also be prepared in a blender.

To cook the pancakes, spray a pancake/shallow sided pan with low calorie cooking spray and heat. Turn down the heat to medium. Pour in enough batter to thinly coat the base of the pan tipping it around from side to side so the base is evenly covered. When the surface of the pancake looks cooked lift the edge with a palette knife to see if the underneath is golden brown. Loosen the edges and flip the pancake over continuing to cook until the other side is golden. Slide onto a plate and cover with foil to keep warm. Repeat this process with the remaining batter.

These are delicious served with lemon juice, sweetener, honey, fresh fruit and yoghurt or as a component to another meal.

Soups

French Onion

Slow Cooked Roasted Vegetable

Spicy Chicken Noodle

Thai Butternut Squash

Winter Warming Parsnip

Spiced Dhal

French Onion

French Onion Soup is really tasty and once you've tried it I'm sure it'll be amongst your must-have recipes. Served with the traditional toasted cheese topping disguises the fact this really is a healthy dish, so serve it to your family, they'll never guess.

Serves 4

low calorie cooking spray, butter flavour

700g onions, peeled, halved and thinly sliced

2 cloves garlic, peeled and crushed

½ teaspoon sweetener (optional)

1.2 litres vegetable stock/water

2 teaspoons yeast extract, marmite etc.

pepper

TOPPING

4 x 15g circles wholemeal bread

4 x 15g portions Gruyere cheese, grated

Coat a large pan with low calorie cooking spray and fry the sliced onions. Cover and cook over a low heat until the onions have softened, stirring from time to time, about 30 minutes. If the pan looks a little dry, add a little more spray. Add the garlic and sweetener (if using) and cook for a further minute.

Stir in the vegetable stock and yeast extract and bring to the boil. Lower the heat, cover the pan and simmer for 30 minutes.

Whilst the soup is cooking prepare the topping. Preheat the grill to high and toast the bread circles on both sides until brown.

When the onions look meltingly soft, season the soup with pepper and ladle into ovenproof bowls. Place the bowls onto a baking tray, top each soup with a toasted bread cirlce and cover each circle with 15g of grated Gruyere cheese. Carefully slide the tray under the grill and cook until the cheese is golden and bubbling, about 2-3 minutes.

Jayne's Tips

For a special first course, substitute the vegetable stock for white wine, which gives the dish a more luxuriant flavour.

Change the Gruyere cheese for Cheddar cheese or Stilton for an alternative flavour.

For a much simpler version, omit the toast and cheese topping and serve 'au natural'!

Slow Cooked Roasted Vegetable

This soup is not only cheap to make but most of the work is done in the oven leaving you time to do other things! If you want to skip the process of roasting the vegetables, then do so by placing them in a pan and cooking in the stock until tender. But be warned, you won't get that lovely roasted flavour coming through.

Serves 8

500g carrots, peeled, cut into chunks

500g celeriac, peeled, cut into chunks

500g leeks, trimmed, washed, halved and cut into chunks

2 onions, peeled and roughly chopped

500g swede, peeled, cut into chunks

3 litres vegetable stock

salt and pepper

handful chopped fresh parsley

1 red chilli, chopped, seeds discarded (optional)

Preheat the oven to 140C/Gas 1.

Place the prepared vegetables into a large ovenproof casserole/pan and add the stock. Bring to a simmer on the hob, then cover and place onto the lowest shelf in the oven. Leave for 3 hours, by which time the vegetables will be meltingly tender.

Pour the vegetables, with the stock, into a blender and blitz until smooth, or use a stick blender directly into the casserole/pan. Once the soup is silky smooth return to the pan and gently reheat until piping hot. Season with a little salt and pepper and serve sprinkled with a little fresh parsley and chilli.

Jayne's Tips

Freeze half of the soup for when time is short and you need something quick and filling.

Spicy Chicken Noodle

This is a take on the traditional chicken noodle soup. If you like your food less spicy just omit or reduce the amount of chilli. It's great for lunch or part of a Thai/Chinese buffet, all healthy of course!

Serves 4

1.4 litres chicken/vegetable stock

5cm piece ginger, peeled and thickly sliced

1 stick lemon grass, trimmed, outer skin removed and halved lengthways

1 red chilli, halved, seeds discarded

5 tablespoons soy sauce

2 tablespoons sweet chilli sauce

4 boned chicken breasts, skinned and all visible fat removed

200g dried rice noodles

6 baby bok choy, sliced

12 basil leaves

12 mint leaves

handful fresh beansprouts (optional)

1 red chilli, thinly sliced into rings, seeds discarded

3 spring onions, trimmed and thinly shredded

2 tablespoons chopped fresh coriander leaves (optional)

To make the soup add the stock, ginger, lemon grass, chilli, soy sauce and sweet chilli sauce to a pan, bring to the boil and reduce to a simmer. Add the chicken, cover and continue to simmer until cooked, about 15 minutes. Remove the chicken, set aside and keep warm. Then remove and discard the ginger, lemon grass and chilli.

Bring back to the boil, add the rice noodles and simmer for 3 minutes or according to the packet instructions. Next add the bok choy and simmer covered for 1 minute. Turn off the heat and leave for a further 2 minutes.

Thickly slice the chicken and add to the serving bowls. Divide the basil, mint and beansprouts (if using) between the bowls and ladle over the soup. Serve garnished with chilli rings, spring onions and sprinkle with coriander.

Thai Butternut Squash

If you're tired of the traditional pumpkin soup then try this recipe. A more pronounced coconut flavour can be achieved using canned light coconut milk but beware this lovely creamy milk comes with added calories, quite addictive really so be warned!

Serves 4

1 onion, peeled and chopped

low calorie cooking spray

2-3 teaspoons green Thai paste (or according to taste)

1 medium butternut squash, peeled, cut into chunks and seeds discarded

400ml Koko coconut milk

salt and pepper

extra milk/stock (optional)

0% Greek yoghurt/low fat fromage frais

fresh coriander leaves, chopped

Fry the onion with the low calorie cooking spray in a medium pan until softened. Then add the green Thai paste and cook for a further 2 minutes.

Add the butternut squash and Koko coconut milk and bring to the boil, cover the pan and simmer until the butternut squash is soft, around 20-30 minutes. Blend until the soup is smooth adding a little salt and pepper to taste. If the soup is too thick add extra milk/stock, reheating as required. Serve garnished with a dollop of yoghurt and sprinkle with coriander leaves.

Jayne's Tips

Koko coconut milk is found in supermarkets alongside the long life milk, or for a less creamy alternative, substitute the milk for vegetable stock.

Winter Warming Parsnip

I LOVE soups. They're filling, nutritious and comforting all in one bowl, which makes them indispensable throughout the year. Plus you can make soup virtually out of anything. I always make double the quantity and freeze some in individual portions for those occasions when I need a hot and satisfying snack ready at my fingertips. No need to ever go hungry.

I like to serve this soup with parsnip crisps. They're quick and easy to make and deliciously crunchy. If you don't fancy making these on the day, prepare them a day ahead and store in an airtight container.

Serves 4

low calorie cooking spray

1 large onion, peeled and roughly chopped

2 garlic cloves, peeled and roughly chopped

1kg parsnips, peeled and roughly chopped

3 star anise (optional)

1.5 litres vegetable stock/water

1½ tablespoons sherry vinegar/white wine vinegar

milk/extra stock for thinning

salt and pepper

FOR THE PARSNIP CRISPS

low calorie cooking spray

1 parsnip, top, tailed and peeled

Preheat the oven to 200C/Gas 6.

In a large pan that has been sprayed with low calorie cooking spray, fry the onion over a medium heat until translucent, about 5-10 minutes. Add the garlic and cook for another minute adding more spray if necessary.

Next, add the parsnips, star anise and stock. Bring to the boil, reduce the heat and simmer until the parsnips are tender, about 20 minutes. Don't be concerned if you notice some scum rising to the surface. This is completely normal and just the cooking process removing the impurities, which can be discarded using a spoon.

Whilst the soup is cooking prepare the parsnip crisps. Spray a large baking tray with the spray, then holding your parsnip down firmly on a chopping board, slice off long ribbon lengths using either a vegetable peeler or a cheese slicer, taking extra care of your fingers as the parsnip gets thinner. Place these 'ribbons' onto the tray, spray again and sprinkle with a little salt. Bake for 10 minutes, then turn the crisps over, spray again and cook for a further 5 minutes. Be careful as the crisps can easily burn. When crisp and golden brown, leave to cool.

Now, back to the soup. Once the parsnips are tender turn off the heat, remove the star anise and add the vinegar. Blend until smooth and return back to the pan adding milk/stock if too thick. Bring back to the boil and simmer for 5 minutes, stirring frequently. Season with a little salt and pepper and serve with any additions (see Jayne's Tips), scattering with parsnip crisps.

Jayne's Tips

Add curry powder, ground cumin or coriander for a spicy parsnip soup, sprinkling over chopped coriander leaves.

Crumble 30g of Stilton cheese into each bowl to make Parsnip and Stilton soup.

Top with sour cream and chive dip (see recipe on p.59) substituting the chives for parsley.

Swirl in a dollop of 0% Greek yoghurt and sprinkle over chopped flat leaf parsley.

Spiced Dhal

By now you'll have guessed that I love soups, but I especially love this one. If you like dhal (of course I mean the healthy version) then you'll love this - it's so satisfying and warming. For those who want extra sustenance then serve with a warm mini naan bread but take into account the extra calories, or opt for a wholemeal roll as a healthier option.

Serves 4 (if you want to share!)

FOR THE SPICE PASTE

2 medium onions, peeled and roughly chopped

3 large garlic cloves, peeled and crushed

1cm piece ginger, peeled and roughly chopped

chilli flakes, to taste (optional)

1 tablespoon ground coriander

1 teaspoon ground cumin

2 teaspoons turmeric

1 teaspoon ground cinnamon

2 tablespoons hot water

low calorie cooking spray

175g red split lentils, washed and drained

175g yellow split peas, washed and drained

1.4 litres water/stock

400g tin chopped tomatoes

salt and pepper

TOPPING

0% Greek yoghurt/low fat fromage frais

sweet chilli sauce (to taste)

Make the spice paste by blending the onion, garlic and ginger together with the spices and hot water in a food processor to form a rough paste, or you could use a pestle and mortar (very satisfying work when you've had an argument!).

Then in a large heavy based saucepan that's been sprayed with low calorie cooking spray cook the paste over a low heat, for about 5 minutes, stirring continuously to avoid it catching and burning.

Stir in the lentils, peas, stock and tomatoes and bring to the boil. Cover the pan and simmer until the peas are tender, about 45 minutes. Add a little extra water if the soup becomes too thick. Season to taste with a little salt and pepper.

For the topping, simply mix together the ingredients and serve dolloped into the middle of each soup. Sit back and enjoy on a cold winter day.

Snacks and Dips

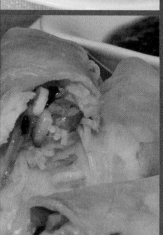

Spring Rolls

Spring rolls are traditionally deep-fried so can be quite oily therefore hiding many unnecessary calories. So, if you'd like to eat them more often, then these recipes maybe for you. There are countless fillings you could use such as Bolognese, Chilli or leftover stir-fried vegetables. You could serve these with a buffet, as a first course, or eaten as part of a Chinese meal.

Makes 4 large or 8 half-size

SPICED PEA AND
POTATO FILLING

300g potatoes cut into small cubes, no need to peel

2 onions, peeled and finely chopped

low calorie cooking spray

2 garlic cloves, peeled and crushed

2-3 teaspoons curry powder
(or to taste)

1 tablespoon black mustard seeds

150g frozen peas, thawed

1 tablespoon water

salt and pepper

2 tablespoons chopped
coriander leaves

TO SERVE

mango chutney

mint raita (see p.60)

salad of your choice

lemon wedges

First prepare the fillings then assemble the spring rolls. Cook the potatoes until just tender, about 5 minutes, then drain. Next, fry the onions in the low calorie cooking spray, cover and cook until soft. Add the garlic, curry powder and mustard seeds and cook for a further minute. Stir in the peas and cooked potato cubes along with 1 tablespoon of water and cook for another minute. Season with a little salt and pepper, turn off the heat and cool. Then stir in the chopped coriander leaves.

Follow the instructions on p.47 for assembling the spring rolls. Serve with mango chutney or mint raita and salad or simply with lemon wedges.

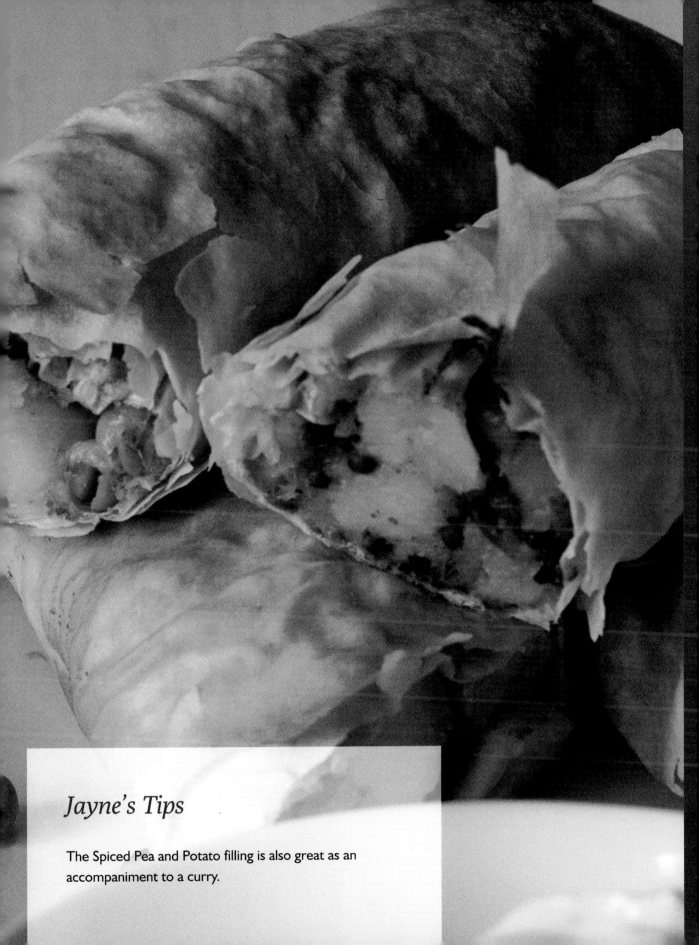

Jayne's Tips

The Spiced Pea and Potato filling is also great as an
accompaniment to a curry.

VEGETABLE FILLING

low calorie cooking spray

1 teaspoon freshly grated ginger

1 clove garlic, peeled and crushed

2 spring onions, trimmed
and shredded

1 red pepper, thinly sliced,
seeds discarded

1 yellow pepper, thinly sliced,
seeds discarded

1 small carrot, peeled, cut in half
and thinly shredded

4 mushrooms, thinly sliced

75g beansprouts

1 tablespoon light soy sauce

TO SERVE

sweet chilli dipping sauce

ASSEMBLING THE SPRING ROLLS

low calorie cooking spray

4 sheets filo pastry

Any vegetable combination works well in this recipe such as bok choy, green beans, mangetout and snow peas. Prawns, diced chicken, shredded lean beef or pork can be added for the meat eaters out there.

Having prepared all the vegetables as above, heat a wok or frying pan with the low calorie cooking spray until hot. Add the ginger, garlic, spring onions, peppers, carrot and mushrooms and cook until beginning to soften, about 2-3 minutes. Next add the beansprouts and soy sauce and cook for a further minute. Turn off the heat and leave to cool.

Follow the instructions below for assembling the spring rolls. This is great served with sweet chilli dipping sauce. Yum!

Preheat the oven to 220C/Gas 7 and spray a baking tray with the low calorie cooking spray.

To make the smaller size simply cut the pastry sheets in half and proceed as below.

Working with one sheet of filo pastry at a time, place a sheet onto a work surface and spray with the cooking spray. Fold in half lengthways so that you have a smaller rectangular shape, turn so the folded edge faces you and spray again. Spoon a quarter of the filling along the length of the pastry leaving a little space at each end. Fold these ends in over the filling and gently roll up starting from the long folded edge. Wet the edge with water and press to seal. Place the roll onto the baking tray and spray well. Repeat with the remaining pastry and filling. Bake until golden brown, about 20 minutes. These rolls can also be cooked in a sprayed frying pan, until golden brown and crisp, turning regularly.

Snacks and Dips

Jayne's Tips

Any leftover filling can be stirred into noodles, pasta or rice for a quick lunch time snack, or even used in an omelette.

When using filo pastry, work with one sheet at a time, covering the remaining sheets with a damp tea towel to prevent them from drying out.

Vietnamese Wraps

What an invention! These Vietnamese wraps are really low in calories and fat, as they are made from tapioca starch and rice flour with added water and salt. Each one weighs just 7g. What I love about these is that you feel as if you're eating a proper wrap. Those of you watching your weight will know exactly what I mean. Once you have made your filling, assembling the wraps is quick and easy. Check out the types of wraps available in supermarkets and Asian food stores.

Makes 8 wraps

FOR THE DRESSING

1 tablespoon rice wine vinegar

2 tablespoons sweet chilli sauce

1 lime, juiced and zest grated

50g fish sauce

1 red chilli, finely chopped, seeds discarded

1 spring onion, trimmed and finely sliced

1 garlic clove, peeled and crushed

2 tablespoons chopped coriander

2 tablespoons chopped mint

FOR THE FILLING

1 carrot, trimmed, peeled and grated

½ cucumber, cut into thin strips

8 soft lettuce leaves, shredded

100g vermicelli noodles, soaked in boiling water for 3-4 minutes, refreshed in cold water and drained well

an assortment cooked prawns, crabsticks or cooked chicken

Mix all the dressing ingredients together in a large bowl. Add the filling and mix together. Set aside.

To assemble the wraps, have ready a plate of warm water. Working with one wrapper at a time, dip it into the water and leave until soft and pliable, about 4 seconds (or according to your packet instructions). Gently remove from the water, drain off any excess and place onto a board or plate.

If using large prawns cut them in half lengthways along the spine creating two halves, removing the thin black intestine. The crabsticks and chicken should be thinly sliced.

Place the filling and your choice of prawns, crabsticks or chicken down the centre of the wrap, leaving a gap at each end for folding. Be careful not to overfill. Fold these ends in so that they cover some of the filling, then take one of the sides, rolling tightly and squeezing together as you roll, being careful not to tear the wrap.

FOR THE ASSEMBLY

8 Vietnamese spring roll wraps

TO SERVE

sweet chilli/hoisin/soy sauce for
dipping or extra dressing

Place on a serving plate whilst you prepare the remaining rolls.
Serve with dipping sauces of your choice.

Jayne's Tips

When using prawns, presentation looks better by taking
two prawn halves, placing them cut-side up along the
centre of the wrap before topping with the filling.

Use lettuce leaves from a soft lettuce rather than from
an iceberg lettuce as this type of lettuce may tear the
wraps.

Thai Vegetable Wraps

These wraps are just great because not only are they easy to make, they are extremely satisfying too and can be varied by filling with almost anything, including leftovers from the fridge (for example vegetables, meat, prawns) making them quite economical and versatile. Serve for a lunch, a picnic or a buffet or accompanying noodles, steamed rice or salad. Unlike the shop bought floury wraps, these are very good on the calorie count, which can be saved up for those special treat occasions. Reduce the amount of Thai paste and chilli according to your taste.

Makes 2 omelettes

low calorie cooking spray

2 peppers, assorted colours, cut into strips, seeds discarded

2 eggs

1 tablespoon light soy sauce

60g canned sweetcorn, drained

1 tablespoon green or red Thai paste

2 spring onions, trimmed and thinly sliced

1 red chilli, finely sliced, seeds discarded

handful beansprouts

small bunch fresh coriander leaves, chopped

sweet chilli sauce/soy sauce for dipping

Preheat the oven to 180C/Gas 4 and spray a baking tray with the low calorie cooking spray.

Place the peppers onto the tray and roast until soft, about 20 minutes or fry in a pan using the spray.

To make the omelettes, beat together the eggs and soy sauce in a small bowl. Heat a frying pan that's been sprayed with low calorie cooking spray, sprinkle half the sweetcorn over the base and then immediately pour in half the egg mixture. Lift the pan off the heat and swirl around so the egg thinly coats the base. Cook until the underneath is set and golden, then carefully flip the omelette over and cook for a further minute. I find it easier to turn over the omelette by covering the pan with a large plate, turning the pan and plate over in one motion so the omelette is on the plate. Then slide the omelette back into the pan. Transfer the cooked omelette to a plate whilst you repeat with the remaining egg mixture.

To assemble, place the omelettes onto a work surface or board. Spread with the Thai paste and fill the centres with the peppers, spring onions, chilli, beansprouts and coriander. Carefully roll up and cut in half diagonally or leave whole and serve with the dipping sauces.

Jayne's Tips

Keep a couple of pre-prepared wraps in the refrigerator for the next day, filling them as and when required.

Baked Potato Stuffed with Crab and Chilli

Baked potatoes are very economical and can be used in many ways such as stuffed with leftovers like chilli, or cut into wedges and baked until golden brown as a healthier alternative to chips. They are even substantial enough as a meal on their own.

As an alternative you could substitute tinned crab with tuna or salmon, or omit the fish altogether. My family frequently enjoy these as a lunchtime meal and if you regularly stock the ingredients it's an ideal dish to quickly serve for friends or family who drop in unexpectedly. Pre-cook the potatoes if you need to save time or if you're caught on the hop, cook first in the microwave finishing off in the oven for a crispy skin. Just remember to spray with low calorie cooking spray before baking.

Serves 1

low calorie cooking spray

1 large baking potato, scrubbed

salt and pepper

1 small can crab in brine, drained

1 tablespoon sweet chilli sauce

2 spring onions, trimmed and sliced

30g Gruyere/Mozzarella cheese, grated

TO SERVE

sweet chilli sauce (optional)

side salad of your choice

Preheat the oven to 200C/Gas 6.

Place the potato onto a baking tray that's been sprayed with low calorie cooking spray and prick with a fork. Spray again, sprinkle with a little salt and bake until a knife inserted through its side penetrates all the way through, about 40-60 minutes. Cool until easy to handle.

Slice off the top and put to one side. Using a teaspoon remove the flesh placing it into a bowl. Then stir in the crab, sweet chilli sauce, spring onions, cheese and a little salt and pepper.

Fill the potato shell with the filling, pressing down firmly, and place onto the baking tray. Place the lid along side, cut side down, and reheat until piping hot, about 10-15 minutes.

Top with its lid and serve with extra sweet chilli sauce and a side salad.

Jayne's Tips

Halve the cooked potatoes, stuff and use as part of a buffet.

Courgette and Mustard Seed Relish

I call this a relish but to be honest it could be eaten as a snack – it's that delicious. It's great served as part of a curry or used as an accompaniment with meat, fish or vegetarian dishes. Make in advance, chill and serve later at room temperature. Low fat Greek yoghurt is great in this recipe as it's thicker than lower fat alternatives plus it tastes a little more luxurious. Leave enough time to salt the courgettes otherwise you won't get the crunch effect.

Serves 4

3 large courgettes, trimmed

salt

2 tablespoons black mustard seeds

500g 0% Greek yoghurt/low fat fromage frais

Prepare the courgettes by grating them using the largest hole on your grater. Transfer to a colander and sprinkle with salt to extract any liquid. Place the colander in a sink or over a bowl to catch any liquid whilst left to rest for at least 30 minutes.

Then using your hands squeeze the courgette flesh quite firmly to extract any remaining liquid. Do this until you have quite a dry mixture (there will be quite a lot of liquid removed).

Heat the mustard seeds in a frying pan that's been sprayed with the low calorie cooking spray until the seeds begin to pop. Stir in the courgettes and cook until quite dry, about 5 minutes. At this point turn off the heat and leave to cool in the pan.

Stir in the yoghurt, transfer to a serving bowl, cover and chill until needed.

Parmesan Crisps

These delicate Parmesan crisps look great when used to garnish savoury dishes or as part of a first course. Be warned they are not only extremely fragile and delicious, but addictive too.

For each crisp you will need:

low calorie cooking spray

1 tablespoon Parmesan cheese, finely grated

adjust quantity to suit size of biscuit cutter

(Pictured on p.144 Butternut Squash Risotto)

Preheat the oven to 170C/Gas 3.

Place a biscuit cutter onto a baking tray that has been sprayed with low calorie cooking spray (use whatever size cutter you have. I use a 6cm cutter). Then, lightly fill the bottom of the cutter with the grated cheese. Carefully remove the cutter and repeat the process for the next crisp. Only make two or three per tray as they cool and harden quickly after baking, making them difficult to remove from the tray. Bake until the crisp is golden brown, about 8-10 minutes. Carefully remove from the tray placing onto a wire rack to cool and firm up. Store in an airtight container until ready to use.

Jayne's Tips

To make curved crisps immediately after baking, drape the crisp over a rolling pin and leave to cool.

My Guilt Free Guacamole

Guacamole is a delicious addition to any meal and traditionally made from avocados. Avocados contain valuable nutrients and healthy fats but it's the FAT that the weight conscious amongst us needs to be cautious of. Now a little fat (especially the healthy ones) isn't bad for you but if you're watching your waistline you can't afford to be eating it on a regular basis.

So bring on the guilt-free guacamole! This version is just as delicious and can be used in exactly the same way. Plus, and here is the big plus, it's good for you and you can eat it regularly.

Makes approximately 200g

150g thawed frozen peas

4 tablespoons fat free fromage frais/ silken tofu

1-2 cloves garlic, peeled and crushed

juice ½ lime

⅛ teaspoon ground cumin

salt and pepper

(Pictured on p.112 My Favourite Store Cupboard Chilli)

To make the guacamole place all the ingredients into a blender and blitz until smooth. Add a little salt and pepper to taste. Refrigerate until ready to serve. It's as simple as that!

I love to serve this with my favourite store cupboard chilli (see recipe on p.111) or use as a dip.

Jayne's Tips

Add chopped fresh chilli and fresh coriander or mint leaves as an alternative.

Sour Cream and Chive Dip

If I had to name one dish that I use regularly and wouldn't be without - this would be it! Calling all these recipes my favourite is becoming a tad repetitive, but honestly, this IS one of my favourites! Did you ever think you'd be able to eat sour cream and chives without feeling guilty?

This is SO good you'll want to eat it whenever and with whatever you want - as a dip, on a jacket potato instead of mayonnaise, stirred into mashed potatoes or on top of chilli. This recipe uses silken tofu which is a product of the soya bean, a wonderful ingredient, containing only 3g of fat per 100g! If you haven't tried soya before, give it a go, you might just like it. But if you're not persuaded, substitute with fat free yoghurt or fromage frais.

---

1 carton silken tofu, found in supermarkets or Asian stores

juice ½ lemon

1-2 cloves garlic, peeled and crushed

a few snipped chives

salt and pepper

This is so simple to make. Just place the silken tofu, lemon juice and garlic into a blender and blitz until smooth. Add the chives and a little salt and pepper, taste and adjust where necessary. Refrigerate until required. 'Voila' there you have it!

Jayne's Tips

The flavour improves with chilling.

Humous

Who would've thought that combining chickpeas, garlic, lemon and fromage frais would result in a delicious and addictive concoction? Use for spreading onto bread or crackers, as a topping on jacket potatoes, a dip served with vegetable crudités, dolloped on top of chilli, simply eaten on its own or as an emergency snack straight from the fridge! It definitely is one of those recipes you want the ingredients readily available to make at a moments notice.

Makes I quantity

400g can chickpeas, rinsed and drained

1-2 cloves garlic, peeled and crushed

lemon juice (to taste)

1-2 tablespoons 0% Greek yoghurt/ low fat fromage frais

salt and pepper (to taste)

Simply place all the ingredients into a blender and blitz together until a paste is formed. If the texture is too stiff add extra fromage frais adjusting the lemon juice, a little salt and pepper and garlic to taste.

Either use straight away or transfer to a container, cover and chill until required.

Jayne's Tips

The flavours will develop if left in the refrigerator.

Mint Raita

If you've eaten in an Indian restaurant, I'm sure you'll have tried mint raita. It's incredibly quick to make at home and can be used in many ways such as a dip, over a jacket potato, a dressing over new potatoes or pasta or simply poured over a bowl of steaming rice or couscous.

Makes 500ml

500ml low fat yoghurt/fromage frais/ silken tofu

3-4 teaspoons mint sauce, no added sugar

sweetener (to taste)

salt (to taste)

Simply mix all of the ingredients together, adjust the seasoning to suit, cover and refrigerate until needed.

(Pictured on p.113 Creamy Potato and Spinach Curry)

Sweet Chilli Dip

I love this dip and use it in endless ways. It can be used as a relish on a burger (delicious), swirled into a soup for a little indulgent kick, or as a low fat dip, accompanied by carrot and pepper sticks. Yum!

Makes 170g

1-2 tablespoons sweet chilli sauce

170g 0% Greek yoghurt/low fat fromage frais

(Pictured on p.42 Spiced Dhal Soup)

Simply blend one tablespoon of the sweet chilli sauce into the yoghurt adding more until you're happy with the flavour, then cover and refrigerate until required. That's it, now enjoy!

Jayne's Tips

Always keep a tub of 0% Greek yoghurt in the refrigerator for times when you just want to knock up something quick, delicious and fat free to nibble on! It's so adaptable.

Curried Dip

Dips are great to have so I think it's worth having at least one in your fridge. Use as a quick snack with vegetable crudités, served over a jacket potato for lunch, as a dressing for pasta or as a topping to spice up a burger. You could substitute curry paste instead of powder but take into account it contains oil.

Makes 500ml

500ml low fat fromage frais/natural yoghurt/soft silken tofu

2 tablespoons mango chutney

2 teaspoons curry powder

salt (to taste)

Simply combine all the ingredients together in a bowl, cover and refrigerate until needed. It's as simple as that!

Frozen Grapes

These grapes taste just like sorbet! Serve as a refreshing snack, as part of a fruit platter or use to garnish other desserts such as mousses, jellies, cheesecakes, fruit tarts..... I could go on forever!

Serves as many as you would like to feed!

Black or green grapes, seedless

Wash the grapes and dry well on kitchen paper. Place onto a tray and freeze overnight. Then store in a freezer bag until required. It's that simple!

Eat straight from the freezer.

Jayne's Tips

Don't let the grapes thaw before eating!

A refreshing treat on a hot day. They have less calories than an ice cream and are much healthier for you too.

Delicious Indulgent Latte

You don't need to visit a coffee house to enjoy a latte when you can make this version at home. Don't reach for the biscuit barrel though - a large slice of guilt-free cheesecake (see recipe on p.191) will do just fine. How much better could it get?

Serves 1

200-250ml skimmed milk

1-2 shots of espresso coffee or a small strong instant coffee

sweetener (to taste)

Start by heating the milk. You could do this in the microwave for 2 minutes, use the steamer attachment on a coffee machine or simply heat in a pan. Prepare the espresso or instant coffee and pour into a mug. Then stir the hot milk into the coffee and vigorously whisk together. Add sweetener to taste and serve piping hot in front of a roaring fire, a girly film and a large slice of cheesecake (guilt-free of course)!

Jayne's Tips

Add a few drops of vanilla extract to the coffee for a vanilla latte or heat the milk with the seeds of half a vanilla pod - just heavenly.

For mocha, dissolve a low fat hot chocolate powder sachet into the latte.

If you own a stick blender, blend some ice cold skimmed milk in a jug until thick and spoon on top for a special treat, believe me it will whip to the consistency of whipped cream. So indulgent!

Add a couple of sugar free syrup shots for that something special.

Fruit Smoothie

Shop bought smoothies, although healthy in appearance, can contain many calories. My version is low in fat and full of flavour. This is great on a summer afternoon, sitting in the sun, watching the world go by.

Serves 1

175g low fat flavoured yoghurt

sugar free flavoured water

crushed ice-cubes

Empty the yoghurt into a blender. Fill the empty tub with flavoured water and add this to the blender. Add crushed ice-cubes and blitz until thick. Pour into a glass, decorate with fruit and drink through a straw.

Fish

Smoked Salmon and Spinach Roulade

How delicious does this dish look? It's brilliant for a summer lunch/evening meal or as a centrepiece to a buffet. Your friends won't believe how you're able to keep so slim and trim eating wonderful food such as this – don't let them know your secret! To vary this recipe you could substitute prawns for the smoked salmon, or for a veggie alternative use boiled and halved quail eggs or lightly cooked mushrooms. This can be prepared the day before, covered and stored in the refrigerator.

Makes 8 good slices

low calorie cooking spray

500g fresh spinach

4 eggs, separated

salt and pepper

freshly grated nutmeg (to taste)

1 tablespoon Parmesan cheese, grated

TO ASSEMBLE

2 tablespoons Parmesan cheese, grated

300g Quark or extra light/light cream cheese

1 tablespoon horseradish cream

fresh dill, chopped (optional)

100g smoked salmon strips

Preheat the oven to 220C/Gas 7 and spray a Swiss roll tin or baking tray with low calorie cooking spray. Line with non-stick baking paper and snip the corners of the paper so that the paper lines the shape of the tin.

Place the spinach into a pan and cook over a low heat until all the liquid has evaporated. Transfer into a food processor and slightly blitz. With the motor running add the egg yolks one at a time, followed by a little salt, pepper, nutmeg and Parmesan cheese. Then turn off the motor, remove the lid and run a spatula around the inside of the bowl so that any stragglers can be incorporated. Replace the lid and blitz for a few more seconds. Transfer to a bowl.

Whisk the egg whites in a grease free bowl until stiff. When the correct consistency has been achieved you'll be able to turn the bowl upside down with the whites staying put! Gradually fold the whites into the spinach mixture. Don't over fold otherwise you'll knock out all of the air. Carefully pour this into the lined tin, persuading it into the corners with a spatula. Again don't be brutal, just gently coax it. Bake until puffed and firm to the touch, about 10-12 minutes.

To assemble have ready a piece of non-stick baking paper and a cooling rack. As soon as the roulade is cooked, remove from the oven and sprinkle it's surface with Parmesan cheese. Lay the paper on top, followed by the rack. With the aid of an oven cloth, hold the tin and rack firmly together and quickly flip over so that the rack is on the bottom.

Remove the tin and lining paper. If the paper is a little stubborn, wet your hand with cold water and rub this over the surface, be careful it'll be hot! The water should create enough steam to allow the paper to lift off without a fight. Once cooled, remove the rack and slide the paper and roulade onto a sheet of tin foil with the longest side facing you.

Then mix together the Quark, horseradish cream and dill (if using). Spread this over the roulade's surface and place the smoked salmon strips in a single line along the roulade's length.

Take hold of the long edge of the paper and in a lifting and pushing motion, roll up to make a Swiss roll shape. When rolled, wrap the roulade in the paper and foil and refrigerate for at least 4 hours to firm up.

Unwrap and serve sliced into 8 pieces (2 per person) for a main meal. Cut into thinner slices if serving as part of a buffet and decorate with lemon slices, smoked salmon and fresh dill.

Jayne's Tips

The quantity of smoked salmon doesn't allow enough strips to completely cover the roulade's surface, so the alternative would be to randomly lay strips over the surface leaving gaps, or increase the quantity of smoked salmon to completely cover.

Monkfish and Prawn Bundles

Filo pastry is so adaptable and this recipe is just one of the ways it can be used. Pastry has always been a 'no no' when watching your weight, but now it can be a 'yes please' when layered with healthier alternatives to butter, oils and creams. If preparing ahead of time, make sure you spray the completed parcels well with the low calorie cooking spray and cover lightly with cling film to prevent them from drying out. Again, substitute the monkfish for salmon, cod or whatever takes your fancy. You could also use a fat free cheese such as Quark or a lighter alternative.

Serves 4

4 x 22.5g sheets filo pastry

low calorie cooking spray, butter flavour

200g skinned and boned monkfish fillet, cut into 2.5cm cubes

200g cooked prawns, thawed and dried on kitchen paper

140g light cream cheese

black pepper

1 tablespoon fresh dill, chopped

juice ½ lemon

TO SERVE

lemon slices and fresh dill to garnish

Preheat the oven to 180C/Gas 4.

To assemble the bundles place one sheet of filo pastry onto a work surface. Cover the remaining sheets with a damp tea towel to prevent them from becoming dry. Spray the sheet of pastry with low calorie cooking spray and fold in half lengthways to form a smaller rectangular shape. Spray again.

Place a quarter of the monkfish in the centre of the pastry. Top with a quarter each of both the prawns and cheese. Season with black pepper, dill and lemon juice.

Gather the pastry into a bundle by bringing up the sides and pressing firmly together in the centre. Transfer the bundle to a small baking tray that has been sprayed with low calorie cooking and spray the pastry again. Repeat with the remaining pastry and filling.

Bake until the pastry is crisp and golden, about 15-20 minutes (allow a couple of extra minutes if coming straight from the refrigerator). Garnish with fresh lemon slices and dill and serve with your favourite vegetables or salads or simply eat as a light lunch or elegant first course.

Salmon and Dill Tarts

These little tarts are really light to eat and are great for picnics, packed lunches or even dinner so the myth that links boring food with healthy eating is just that – a myth.

Use any combination of fish in these little tarts.

Serves 6

FOR THE FILLING

150ml skimmed milk

2 eggs

salt and pepper

6 asparagus spears

200g fresh salmon fillet, skinned (all bones removed)

sprig of fresh dill, chopped

FOR THE PASTRY SHELLS

low calorie cooking spray, butter flavour

6 sheets filo pastry

6 muffin moulds or ramekins

Preheat the oven to 180C/Gas 4.

For the filling mix together the milk, eggs and a little salt and pepper. Snap off the bottom end of each asparagus spear and discard. Slice the spears into small rounds leaving the tip whole. Chop the salmon into 18 small chunks.

Place the moulds onto a baking tray and line each with the pastry. Work with one sheet of pastry at a time making sure you cover the other sheets with a damp tea towel to prevent them from drying out. Cut the pastry sheet into four equal pieces and then spray with low calorie cooking spray. Place the pastry pieces on top of one another to form a star shape. Pick up the shape and ease into the mould pushing carefully so as not to tear it. Repeat with the remaining pastry until the six moulds have been lined. Then spray again.

Fill the pastry shells each with three pieces of salmon followed by the asparagus and dill. Pour in the milk/egg mixture and bake until golden and set, about 20-30 minutes.

Jayne's Tips

Silicone muffin moulds work really well as they don't need greasing. If you'd prefer to use a tin, make sure you grease it with low calorie cooking spray before adding the pastry to prevent it from sticking.

These tarts can be made in a variety of sizes. A large one would make a great centre-piece whereas mini tarts make perfect canapés.

Marinated Thai Baked Salmon

This spectacular dish is great for a buffet, special occasion or a family gathering. Any leftovers can be used in noodles or pasta, cold with salad or simply eaten in a sandwich. It's so incredibly easy to prepare but if time is short use the ready prepared Thai paste available in supermarkets. Salmon portions are also a great alternative rather than buying a whole side of salmon. You could also substitute colely or cod for the salmon.

Serves 6-8

FOR THE THAI PASTE

2 lemongrass stalks

120ml dark soy sauce

1 bunch fresh coriander, leaves reserved, stalks finely chopped

2.5cm piece fresh ginger, peeled and finely grated

4 garlic cloves, peeled and crushed

FOR THE SALMON

1kg fresh salmon fillet, skinned

4 tablespoons honey (optional)

TO SERVE

2 red chillies, finely sliced, seeds discarded

4 spring onions, finely sliced

2 limes, cut into quarters

Make the Thai paste by cutting the base and top off the lemongrass stalks. Bash the stalks with a rolling pin or use a pestle and mortar to break down the fibres. Finely chop the stalks and mix them together with the soy sauce, coriander stalks, ginger and garlic.

Place the salmon fillet in a large plastic food bag and pour in the paste. Gently rub this over the salmon flesh and place the bag onto a tray. Leave to marinate for an hour or so in the refrigerator.

Preheat the oven to 200C/Gas 6.

Remove the salmon from the marinade and place onto a baking tray lined with tin foil. Drizzle over the honey (if using) and bake until cooked (about 15-20 minutes depending upon the thickness of your fillet). You can check it's cooked by gently piercing the centre of the fillet with a knife. If it looks red bake for another 5 minutes, then check again.

Transfer to a serving plate and sprinkle with the sliced chillies, spring onions and reserved coriander leaves. Squeeze over the limes and serve with a simple salad, a few noodles or with roasted baby new potatoes and steamed vegetables.

Who doesn't like Fish Pie?

Fish Pie is such a popular dish. I normally make this the day before and pop it into the oven after a long day at work. Fish needs very little cooking otherwise it becomes tough and dry, which is why there's no need to pre-cook it in this recipe. The longest procedure here is to peel the potatoes and make the sauce, which can all be done ahead of time. Substitute for any fish you like such as Coley (if you're on a budget), add king prawns or langoustines, scallops or even mussels, whatever your purse allows. Look out for special deals in supermarkets offering frozen seafood, ready at hand to make this dish even easier, more affordable and maybe even a little bit exotic too. But be warned, NEVER use seafood that has previously been frozen if you're planning to freeze ahead, ONLY use fresh seafood in this case. No upset tummies please!

Serves 4

15g dried mushrooms

1 quantity white sauce, made with fish stock and the reserved soaking liquid taken from the mushrooms, (see recipe for white sauce on p.177)

500g fresh fish such as cod, salmon etc. skinned, cut into chunks

a handful of raw prawns (optional)

salt and pepper

low calorie cooking spray

1kg potatoes, peeled and cut into large chunks

2 egg yolks

150ml skimmed milk

freshly grated nutmeg

Preheat the oven to 180C/Gas 4.

Place the dried mushrooms into a bowl and cover with boiling water. Leave for 20 minutes to soften. Then, strain the liquid, keeping for the white sauce. Finely chop the mushrooms.

Prepare the white sauce using fish stock and the reserved mushroom liquid (see recipe on p.177).

Mix together the fish chunks, prawns and a little salt and pepper and place into a medium sized ovenproof dish sprayed with low calorie cooking spray.

Once prepared, fry the chopped mushrooms in a small pan until soft. Then stir in the white sauce and pour over the fish.

For the potato topping, boil the potatoes until tender, drain and return back to the pan, add a little salt and pepper, egg yolks and milk. Mash well and either spoon or pipe onto the fish, sprinkling with a little grated nutmeg. Bake until golden brown and bubbling, about 30-40 minutes, allowing an extra 5-10 minutes if the pie comes straight from the refrigerator.

This is best served piping hot with fresh vegetables.

Jayne's Tips

For a special touch make these in individual dishes.

When the pie has been prepared, instead of cooking it you can cover and refrigerate overnight.

Spicy Fish Parcels

Salmon has become an affordable fish these days, making this dish suitable for family meals or as a tasty course when entertaining. As an alternative, substitute it with any firm fleshed fish. If you like your meals milder or are catering for someone who dislikes spicy food, it's easy to tailor each parcel according to individual tastes.

Serves 4

1 teaspoon turmeric

1 teaspoon ground cumin

4 teaspoons wholegrain mustard

salt and pepper

4 skinless/boneless fish fillets
(see above)

2.5cm chunk ginger, peeled and sliced

1 clove garlic, peeled

1 bunch fresh coriander, washed

2 red/green chillies, sliced,
seeds discarded

200ml fat free 0% Greek yoghurt/
low fat fromage frais

fresh coriander leaves,
chopped (optional)

sliced chilli rings, seeds discarded
(optional)

Preheat the oven to 220C/Gas 7.

Prepare the spice rub by mixing together the turmeric, cumin, mustard and a little salt and pepper. Rub over the fish and transfer to a plate.

Place the ginger, garlic, coriander and chillies in a blender and blitz. Add the yoghurt and blitz again. Spread this over the fish, cover and refrigerate for at least 30 minutes.

When ready to cook, take four sheets of tin foil and place a piece of fish into the middle of each sheet. Gather up the sides and seal the edges together to make four parcels, not too tight as the steam won't be able to circulate and keep the fish nice and moist whilst it cooks.

Place the parcels onto a baking tray and bake until cooked, about 8-10 minutes. To check if it's cooked, open a parcel and make a small cut into the centre of the fillet. If it's still red, cook for a little longer.

Remove the foil and serve garnished with coriander leaves and chilli rings, accompanied with vegetables or salad and either steamed rice, new potatoes or noodles.

Jayne's Tips

If you're making parcels with different fillings don't forget to mark the foil with a black marker pen so they can easily be identified.

Better than Avocado and Prawns

Avocado pear is such a delicious fruit. Its texture is meltingly soft and it has a smooth, buttery flavour. Unfortunately it contains fat – albeit healthy fat but when you're watching your shape you don't want to watch it expand! Substituting papaya for the avocado may seem strange but believe me, it's delicious. If you like this version there's no reason why it couldn't be eaten as often as you wish. Unlike the avocado, a papaya's flesh will not discolour once exposed to the air, which is an added bonus. You could substitute low fat mayonnaise for the yoghurt/fromage frais but in my opinion it's not necessary, it tastes just as yummy as it is.

Serves 4

2 ripe papayas

2 limes juiced

4 tablespoons 0% Greek yoghurt/low fat fromage frais

I teaspoon tomato ketchup

a few drops Worcestershire sauce

salt and pepper

200g cooked prawns, thawed if frozen

TO SERVE

dill or fennel fronds (optional)

4 large cooked prawns (optional)

First cut the papaya in half horizontally. Remove and discard the black seeds with a teaspoon and pour over the lime juice. Set aside.

To make the dressing, mix together the yoghurt, tomato ketchup and Worcestershire sauce. Season with a little salt and pepper, then stir in the prawns.

When ready to serve fill the papaya with the prawn mixture and garnish with the dill and the extra prawns.

Meat and Poultry

Beef Balti

Let's face it, takeaways are not only delicious but also convenient and there's nothing wrong in indulging in them once in a blue moon. Unfortunately they contain hidden calories in the form of fat! So why not make your own without the massive fat content. It's much better for your health and waistline, and you'll be able to enjoy a homemade 'takeaway' as frequently as your heart desires. Why not combine with one or two vegetable curries, rice and a mint raita (see recipes on p.113, p.119 and p.60) for the complete 'curry night-in' minus the guilt factor. The cooking times are only a guide and the beef should be cooked until it's really tender.

Serves 4

1kg lean cubed stewing beef

low calorie cooking spray

1 onion, peeled and thinly sliced

2 garlic cloves, peeled and chopped

2 tablespoons balti spice powder

1 teaspoon garam masala

a few curry leaves, fresh if possible (optional, available in supermarkets or Asian stores)

4 tomatoes, roughly chopped or 400g can chopped tomatoes

500ml beef stock

2 tablespoons tomato puree

1 medium sized butternut squash, washed, halved, cut into chunks, seeds discarded (no need to peel)

fresh coriander leaves, chopped

Fry the beef in batches with the low calorie cooking spray. I find a deep-sided pan does the job nicely. Once browned, remove from the pan and set aside.

Add the sliced onions to the pan and fry, adding more spray if necessary. Cover and cook over a medium heat until softened. Add the garlic and cook for a further minute, then stir in the balti spice powder, garam masala and curry leaves. Cook for a minute longer.

Return the beef to the pan with the remaining ingredients excluding the fresh coriander. Bring to the boil, cover the pan and simmer until the beef is really tender, about 1-1½ hours. Sprinkle with the chopped coriander leaves and serve with rice, a vegetable curry or any accompaniment of your choice.

Jayne's Tips

Make the day before and chill, then reheat until piping hot.

Beef Bourguignon

Once upon a time this dish appeared on most restaurant menus. Hopefully, after trying this version, it will appear regularly in your repertoire. Allow plenty of time to cook the meat. Cooking time should be according to the time it takes your meat to reach that meltingly soft stage. The timings in my recipe are only a guide. What you're aiming for is meat that's as soft as velvet rather than a chewy chunk you can't swallow but your pet dog would love you for! It's also worth keeping an eye on the liquid in the pan, as you may need to add a little extra stock along the way, so you're left with a lovely rich sauce at the end. One little tip is to place a circle of greaseproof paper over the contents of the pan, before you pop the lid on. This will help conserve the lovely juices whilst the beef slowly cooks.

Serves 4

FOR THE BOURGUIGNON

low calorie cooking spray

1kg lean stewing beef, cubed

60g lean bacon, sliced

1 onion, peeled and sliced

1 carrot, peeled and sliced

2 cloves garlic, peeled and crushed

1 dessertspoon flour

350ml red wine (optional) or use water/beef stock

1 beef stock cube/300ml water

1 tablespoon tomato puree

½ teaspoon dried thyme or 1 teaspoon fresh

1 bouquet garni

500g baby onions

240g mushrooms, quartered

salt and pepper

1 tablespoon parsley, chopped

Preheat the oven to 180C/Gas 4.

In a large pan that's been sprayed with low calorie cooking spray, fry the beef cubes on all sides, removing them to a plate as they brown. Do this in batches if necessary to avoid overcrowding otherwise the meat will steam rather than brown. Fry the bacon in the same pan for a minute, adding the onion, carrot and garlic, cooking for a further minute.

Return all the meat to the pan with any juices that have collected on the plate. Then add the flour and mix to coat the meat. Add the wine, stock cube and water, tomato puree, thyme and bouquet garni. Cover with a paper disc (see recipe introduction) and the lid and cook in the oven until the meat is tender. This may take 1-2 hours.

Whilst the meat is cooking prepare the baby onions by placing them unpeeled onto a sprayed baking tray. Roast until they begin to soften, about 20-30 minutes, and set aside to cool. Then cut off the stalk end and peel away the skin.

Next fry the mushrooms in the spray until tender and leave to cool.

Once the meat is cooked, remove the bouquet garni, stir in the onions and mushrooms and reheat until piping hot. Season to taste with a little salt and pepper, sprinkle with parsley and serve with mashed, boiled potatoes or gratin Dauphinoise and red cabbage and apple, (see recipes on p.95, p.173 and p.171) or any other vegetable that tickle your fancy.

Jayne's Tips

Instead of cooking in the oven you could cook very gently on the stove.

Ragu

A basic Ragu sauce is one of those essential staples which busy working mums, dads and singletons can have to hand. If time permits, double or triple the recipe, divide into portions and freeze. It's then ready to use at a moments notice in dishes such as Bolognese, Chilli and Shepherd's Pie to name but a few. Its uses are endless.

Serves 4

1 onion, peeled and finely chopped

low calorie cooking spray

2 carrots, peeled and finely chopped

2 cloves garlic, peeled and crushed

500g extra lean beef/lamb/ vegetarian mince

400g can chopped tomatoes

500g carton passata

1 tablespoon dried oregano or 2 tablespoons fresh oregano

2 handfuls chopped fresh basil

2 tablespoons balsamic vinegar

4 tablespoons tomato puree

salt and pepper

Fry the onions in the low calorie cooking spray over a gentle heat until transparent. Add the carrots and cook for a further 3 minutes, followed by the garlic and cook a minute longer. Add the mince and cook until browned, breaking up with a wooden spoon. Then stir in the remaining ingredients with the exception of the salt and pepper and bring to the boil. Reduce the heat, cover and simmer stirring occassionally until the sauce has thickened, about 30 minutes. Add a little water if the sauce starts to stick. Season with a little salt and pepper.

Variations:

FOR SPAGHETTI BOLOGNESE

Add 240g of sliced mushrooms 10 minutes before the end of cooking. Serve with spaghetti and a grating of Parmesan cheese.

FOR CHILLI CON CARNE

Add a 400g can of drained red kidney beans, 2 teaspoons each of ground cumin and ground coriander and 1 teaspoon of chilli powder (or according to taste) plus 1 chopped red chilli (with or without seeds). Serve with rice and a crisp salad.

FOR SHEPHERD'S PIE

Throw in some frozen peas and pour into an ovenproof dish. Spread or pipe mashed potato on top and cook in a preheated oven, 180C/Gas 4, until piping hot and golden brown, about 30 minutes. Serve with vegetables of your choice.

Jayne's Tips

Make the mashed potato for the Shepherd's Pie using half potato and half cooked swede and carrots for a delicious alternative.

Peppered Steak

Select any cut of steak you fancy and cook according to how rare you like it. It's great with potato wedges or fluffy mashed potatoes, teamed with a mushroom or red wine sauce (see recipes on p.172, p.95, p.178 and p.179). Serve with a crisp green salad, grilled mushrooms and tomatoes, maybe even peas. It sounds like a restaurant meal doesn't it? Healthier by far though.

Serves 4

2 tablespoons black peppercorns, coarsely ground

4 teaspoons Dijon mustard

4 x 175g sirloin steaks

salt

low calorie cooking spray

Place the black peppercorns in an even layer over a small plate. Then spread half teaspoon of Dijon mustard over one side of each steak. Press the steaks into the peppercorns, ensuring the peppercorns stick and sprinkle with a little salt. Repeat on the other side and set aside.

In a frying pan that's been sprayed with low calorie cooking spray cook the steaks according to your preference. Take care not to move the steaks around the pan too much otherwise the peppercorns will fall off. Once cooked let the steaks rest for 1-2 minutes before serving. This allows any juices to retract back into the meat making the steaks more succulent.

Serve with any sides you fancy.

Jayne's Tips

Depending on the thickness of the steaks, cook for about
2 minutes on each side for rare, about 3 minutes for
medium and about 5 minutes for well done.

Fillet Steak with a Trio of Mushrooms

This is delicious served when entertaining friends or simply for a special family gathering. It can be prepared in advance and chilled, allowed to come back to room temperature and simply popped into the oven just before serving.

Serves 4

300ml boiling water

30g dried mushrooms

low calorie cooking spray

1 small onion, peeled and finely chopped

1-2 garlic cloves, peeled and chopped

100g wild mushrooms, trimmed and chopped

125g chestnut mushrooms, chopped

2 tablespoons dry white wine or beef stock

1 tablespoon finely chopped thyme

salt and pepper

4 tablespoons low fat cream

1 egg yolk (optional)

2 tablespoons Parmesan cheese, grated

4 x 175g fillet steaks, (4-5cm thick)

Preheat the oven to 220C/Gas 7.

Pour 300ml boiling water over the dried mushrooms and leave for 30 minutes to hydrate. Drain and finely chop the mushrooms, keeping the liquid for later.

In a pan that's been sprayed with low calorie cooking spray cook the chopped onion until softened. Add the garlic and cook for a further minute. Next add the wild and chestnut mushrooms and fry until brown, adding more spray if necessary. Add the white wine and reserved mushroom liquid and cook until completely reduced. Stir in the thyme, a little salt and pepper and cream and cook until the mixture is dry and the cream coats the mushrooms. Transfer to a bowl, leave to cool and then stir in the egg yolk and Parmesan cheese.

Fry the steaks in the spray until brown all over, about 2-3 minutes. Turn off the heat and transfer to a shallow baking tray. Top each steak with the mushroom mixture. The steaks can be covered and chilled at this stage if you're preparing this dish ahead of time.

Cook the steaks in the oven for 10-12 minutes for medium-rare (depending upon their thickness and how rare you like your steak) until the topping is golden and bubbling. Remove from the oven, cover with foil and let stand for a couple of minutes. Serve with a crisp green salad or fresh vegetables and jacket wedges.

Jayne's Tips

The internal temperatures for cooked steak are:
medium-rare 60C
medium 71C
well-done 77C

Lamb Shanks in a Red Wine Sauce

Lamb shanks are delicious and extremely satisfying, plus if they're cooked properly the meat falls off the bone. Served with a mound of fluffy mashed potatoes and fresh vegetables, this can pass as a family meal or as a delicious course to be served to guests. It tastes even better if made the day before and refrigerated overnight as it allows the flavours to develop. It can also be frozen for use at a later date when time is pressing.

Serves 4

low calorie cooking spray

4 lamb shanks, all visible fat removed

2 red onions, peeled and finely sliced

1 whole garlic bulb, cloves separated but skins left on

1 teaspoon dried rosemary or 2 fresh rosemary sprigs

400g can chopped tomatoes

142ml red wine or substitute with lamb/chicken stock

200ml lamb/chicken/vegetable stock

2 dessertspoons balsamic vinegar

salt and pepper

Preheat your oven to 180C/Gas 4.

Then, in an ovenproof dish that's been sprayed with low calorie cooking spray, cook the lamb shanks until brown on all sides. Once browned, remove from the dish and place onto a plate.

Next add the sliced onions to the dish, adding more spray if required, and cook until golden brown and turning soft. Then add the garlic cloves and cook for a further minute.

Return the lamb shanks to the dish with the rosemary sprigs, chopped tomatoes, red wine, stock and any juices that have accumulated on the plate and bring to the boil.

Cover the dish and place in the oven, cooking until the meat is tender and starting to fall off the bone, about 2-2½ hours. Then add the balsamic vinegar and season with a little salt and pepper to taste.

Serve immediately with mashed potatoes or mashed swede and carrot puree and seasonal vegetables or cool, cover and refrigerate until required.

Jayne's Tips

If made the day before and refrigerated overnight, any fat will have risen to the surface and can be spooned off and discarded.

If you don't have a dish that can be used both on the hob and inside the oven, use a frying pan to fry the lamb and onions then transfer these into an ovenproof dish.

If oven space is a problem cook directly on the hob, over a very low heat, for a couple of hours until the lamb is just about to fall off the bone.

Sausage and Mash with Onion Gravy

Yum is all I can say. This truly is comfort food without the guilt. I love puddles of gravy with my mash so I've doubled the ingredients for the gravy, but you can halve the quantities if this is not the case for you. It's important to note that this recipe contains raw egg yolk, so omit if pregnant or if you have a medical condition where you cannot eat raw eggs (please refer to the section 'About the Ingredients' for information on raw eggs).

Serves 4

8 low fat sausages

low calorie cooking spray

4 red onions, peeled and cut into wedges

2 thyme sprigs

salt and pepper

FOR THE HONEY ROASTED CARROTS WITH ORANGE

1 bunch carrots (about 10-12)

1 orange, zest grated

1 tablespoon honey

FOR THE MASHED POTATOES

1.5 kg potatoes, peeled

1 egg yolk

150ml skimmed milk

FOR THE ONION GRAVY

a couple of splashes of red wine vinegar or balsamic vinegar

400ml vegetable stock

Preheat the oven to 200C/Gas 6.

Place the sausages into a roasting tin that's been sprayed with low calorie cooking spray. Add the onion wedges, thyme sprigs and a little salt and pepper and roast for 20 minutes. Remove from the oven, give it a good mix and spray again. Roast for a further 10-20 minutes until the sausages are nicely browned. Keep warm.

For the honey roasted carrots, top and tail the carrots and scrub well (no need to peel). Place into an ovenproof dish, spray, sprinkle over the orange zest, drizzle with honey and a little salt and pepper. Roast until just tender, about 20-30 minutes. Keep warm.

For the mashed potatoes cut the potatoes into pieces of equal size and place into a saucepan. Cover with water and bring to the boil. Simmer over a medium heat until soft and then drain. Mash in the pan with a potato masher or ricer. Add the egg yolk, milk and a little salt and pepper. Mix well and keep warm.

For the onion gravy, remove the sausages from the tin, add the vinegar to the onions and cook until most of it has bubbled away. Add the stock and simmer until reduced by half, stirring from time to time, then season to taste with a little salt and pepper. Just before serving return the sausages to the tin and warm through.

Jayne's Tips

For a special occasion, spend a little extra time piping the potatoes into fluffy rosettes, called Duchesse Potatoes. To do this place the mashed potato into a piping bag fitted with a large star nozzle. Onto a baking tray that's been sprayed with low calorie cooking spray, pipe rosettes (approximately 10-15cm diameter). If they are not to your liking, don't worry scoop the potato off and pipe again. Refrigerate for 30 minutes or overnight. Just before cooking, add seasoning to a beaten egg yolk and use to very gently brush the rosettes. Refrigerate for 10 minutes then brush again. Bake for 20 minutes until piping hot and golden.

Chilli Sausages with Potato Topping

This is a great all-round family favourite, plus it's really easy to prepare. This recipe uses canned chilli beans that are readily available in most supermarkets. These are kidney beans in a tasty, but not spicy-hot, sauce. You can substitute ordinary canned kidney beans if you prefer but add a can of chopped tomatoes or a carton of passata as well.

Serves 4

1 large onion, peeled, halved and thinly sliced

low calorie cooking spray

8 of your favourite low fat sausages

2 x 400g cans chilli beans

salt and pepper

500g potatoes, unpeeled, scrubbed and thinly sliced

Preheat the oven to 180C/Gas 4.

Fry the sliced onion in a large ovenproof dish that's been sprayed with low calorie cooking spray, cover and cook over a low heat until softened, about 5-10 minutes. Add the garlic and cook for a further minute.

Cut the sausages into chunks and add them in batches to the softened onion and cook until golden brown. Return all the sausages back to the dish stirring in the chilli beans and a little salt and pepper.

Next, layer the potato slices over the top, spray well and sprinkle with a little salt and pepper. Place on a baking tray and cook in the oven until the potatoes are golden brown, about 50-60 minutes. Serve with a salad or vegetables of your choice.

Meat and Poultry

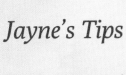

Jayne's Tips

If you're preparing this dish in advance, to prevent the potatoes discolouring place the potato slices into a pan of boiling water and cook for 2 minutes. Drain and rinse under cold water. Assemble as above, cover the dish with cling film and refrigerate until required.

I Don't Believe it's Coronation Chicken

This is one of those dishes that's hard to distinguish from the real deal and yet it's so healthy. This version uses low fat fromage frais instead of the traditional full fat mayonnaise and the result is amazing. I'll be surprised if your nearest and dearest can tell the difference.

Serves at least 6 depending on portion size or 1 hungry person who doesn't want to share!

500g low fat fromage frais

1-2 tablespoons mango chutney (or to taste)

curry powder (to taste)

salt and pepper

1kg cooked chicken, all skin removed

240g grapes, washed and halved

fresh parsley, chopped

In a large bowl mix together the fromage frais, mango chutney, curry powder and a little salt and pepper.

Cut the cooked chicken into bite size pieces and add these to the bowl. Stir well to ensure all the chicken is thoroughly coated. Add the halved grapes and stir once more. Chill in the refrigerator until ready to serve, sprinkled with parsley.

Jayne's Tips

This is perfect for a picnic, as part of a buffet, or the leftovers can be stirred into pasta.

Green Thai Chicken Salad

If you enjoyed the recipe for Coronation Chicken on p.99 then you'll love this salad. Again it's so simple to make and if time is short you can buy a Thai paste (either red or green) in supermarkets that will make the job even easier. Be aware however that shop-bought versions contain some oil so take into account the extra calories. This is a lovely dish for a picnic or a summer time evening supper. Enjoy.

Serves 4-6

FOR THE GREEN THAI PASTE

1 small green chilli

2 spring onions, trimmed and washed

1cm ginger, peeled

½ teaspoon black peppercorns

2 garlic cloves, peeled

2 tablespoons fresh coriander leaves, chopped

1 lemon grass stalk, ends and outer covering removed

1 lemon, zest finely grated

½ teaspoon ground cumin

½ teaspoon ground coriander

½ teaspoon salt

½ teaspoon fish sauce

low calorie cooking spray

FOR THE SALAD

500g 0% Greek yoghurt/low fat fromage frais

1 tablespoon mango chutney

salt and pepper

1kg cooked (or leftover) chicken, chopped into bite size pieces

Prepare the paste by blending all of the ingredients with the exception of the cooking spray together in a food processor. Then cook the paste in a frying pan that's been sprayed with low calorie cooking spray over a medium heat for about 2 minutes, stirring constantly to prevent from sticking. Remove from the heat and let it cool in the pan.

To make the salad, stir the yoghurt and chutney together with a little salt and pepper and mix into the cooled Thai paste. Pour this over the chicken making sure it's coated, cover and refrigerate for at least an hour so that the flavours can develop.

This is great served with a couscous salad, such as mango and chilli, a bean and Quinoa salad (see recipes on p.153 and p.169), or with new potatoes sprinkled with mint and a fresh tomato and basil salad. Summer on a plate!

Chicken with Caramelised Red Onions

Chicken is one of those products which is great to cook with, as there are countless ways it can be used. However, it can also become bland and boring, unless you get creative with sauces, seasonings and herbs to turn it into something more interesting and tasty. Be warned though, the skin contains enormous amounts of fat, so by removing it you instantly remove a large quantity of unwanted calories, making poultry a low fat component to any meal. This dish is very easy to prepare and super healthy too - an added bonus. My family find chicken cooked this way exceptionally scrummy, so it's become a Saturday evening favourite in our household. Have fun experimenting with different flavour combinations to create your own favourite.

Serves 4

500g red onions, peeled and thinly sliced

low calorie cooking spray

2 cloves garlic, peeled and crushed

½ tablespoon fresh rosemary, chopped

1 teaspoon honey

juice and finely grated zest 1 orange

4 large chicken breasts, skinned

salt and pepper

1 tablespoon fresh parsley, chopped

Preheat the oven to 180C/Gas 4.

Place the sliced onions in a large pan that's been sprayed with low calorie cooking spray, cover and cook over a low heat until soft and brown, about 20-30 minutes. Stir from time to time and if they begin to stick add a little more spray. Be patient otherwise they may burn and taste bitter. Then add the garlic, rosemary, honey, orange juice and zest and cook for a further 2 minutes.

Spray a shallow ovenproof dish and add the chicken breasts. Spread the onion mixture over the chicken, season with a little salt and pepper and bake until cooked and the juices run clear, about 30-40 minutes. Serve sprinkled with chopped parsley and accompanied by vegetables or a salad of your choice.

Jayne's Tips

Prepare in advance by cooking the topping, cool completely and spread over the raw chicken. Cover and refrigerate overnight. Add an extra 5-10 minutes cooking time if cooking straight from the fridge.

Goats' Cheese and Pesto Stuffed Chicken

If you're one of those people who absolutely hate goats' cheese, I forgive you. I personally love it. If you're of that inclination then you can substitute it in this recipe with a low fat soft cheese or cheese triangles. For that extra special dinner swap the pesto with garlic and add Parma ham instead of bacon. Serve as a main course or cook, chill, slice and serve cold on a platter for a buffet, picnic or lunch – so much choice!

Serves 4

4 large chicken breasts, skinned

4 x 35g soft goats' cheese

4 teaspoons roasted red pepper pesto

8 bacon rashers, all visible fat removed

low calorie cooking spray

pepper

Preheat the oven to 180C/Gas 4.

Make a horizontal incision along the length of each chicken breast cutting three-quarters of the way through to form a pocket. Place a portion of the goats' cheese inside each pocket topped with a teaspoon of pesto. Press the cut edges together to seal and wrap two rashers of bacon around each breast to enclose the filling. Place onto an ovenproof dish that's been sprayed with low calorie cooking spray, season with pepper and spray again. (These can be covered and chilled at this stage if preparing the dish in advance).

Bake until the chicken is tender and the juices run clear, about 30-40 minutes, depending on the thickness of the chicken, adding 5-10 minutes to the cooking time if the chicken comes straight from the refrigerator.

Serve with roasted baby new potatoes and seasonal vegetables or a crisp green salad.

Chinese Duck

Cooked duck has extremely rich and fatty skin. If you remove the skin you'll instantly remove the fat. If you're a fan of traditional Peking duck, and I'm one of those, you may well love this recipe as it can be used in a similar way. Serve the duck shredded and wrapped in large lettuce leaves, like iceberg, for a fresh and healthy alternative to Peking duck wraps. You could accompany it with delicious stir-fried vegetables (using low calorie cooking spray of course) and a bowl of steaming noodles for a fantastic Chinese meal. Yum! Much better than a greasy, sweet, sickly Chinese takeaway any day.

Serves 4

8 tablespoons hoisin sauce

2 teaspoons Chinese five-spice powder

4 duck breasts, skin and all fat removed

low calorie cooking spray

TO SERVE

soy sauce/extra hoisin sauce

Prepare the marinade by combining the hoisin sauce and Chinese five-spice powder together in a small mixing bowl then brush this over the duck breasts. Place onto a plate, cover with cling film and refrigerate for at least 30 minutes.

When ready to cook, heat a frying pan that's been sprayed with low calorie cooking spray and add the duck. Cook for about 5 minutes until browned. Turn them over, cooking for another 2-3 minutes, for medium-rare, until the bottom is brown and the flesh is springy to the touch, longer if you want them well done. Remove from the heat, cover with foil to keep warm and rest for about 5 minutes. Slice diagonally and serve with soy sauce or extra hoisin sauce and any accompaniments that take your fancy.

Jayne's Tips

As an alternative, you can serve the duck cold as part of a salad or hot added to noodles or pasta.

Vegetarian

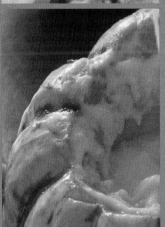

Stuffed Pumpkin with Wild Mushrooms

I never tire of pumpkin, but I know some people do. If this sounds like you, try this version for a change. It tastes delicious and is incredibly filling.

**Serves 2 as a main course or
4 as a side dish or first course**

low calorie cooking spray

1 butternut squash, washed

25g dried mushrooms

1 onion, peeled and finely chopped

2 cloves garlic, peeled and crushed

110g wild mushrooms, chopped

250g mushrooms, chopped

4 tablespoons low fat single cream

2 thyme sprigs

salt and pepper

TOPPING

60g Gruyere cheese, grated (optional)

Preheat the oven to 180C/Gas 4 and spray a baking tray with low calorie cooking spray.

Prepare the butternut squash by cutting off the top. Then cut in half lengthways and using a teaspoon, remove and discard the seeds and any membrane. Place the squash onto the tray, spray well and bake until just tender, about 30-40 minutes.

Place the dried mushrooms into a bowl and cover with boiling water. Leave to hydrate for about 30 minutes. Drain, reserving the liquid, and finely chop.

Prepare the filling by frying the onion in a sprayed pan until softened. Add the garlic and cook for a further minute. Then add the chopped and hydrated mushrooms and both types of fresh mushrooms and cook until soft and reduced in size, about 10 minutes. Sieve over the reserved mushroom liquid (to remove any grit that may have been present with the dried mushrooms) and cook until almost evaporated.

Add the cream, thyme and a little salt and pepper and stir. Cook gently until the cream just coats the mushrooms, 1-2 minutes.

Once the squash is cooked fill the hollows with the filling and bake until piping hot, about 10-15 minutes. Sprinkle with the cheese and cook until golden brown, another 5 minutes or so. Serve accompanied by a green salad and beetroot and pear salad (see recipe on p.151) or serve as a vegetable accompaniment to meat, fish or chicken.

Jayne's Tips

For a tasty alternative chop 4 rashers of bacon (all fat removed) and cook in low calorie cooking spray until crispy. Then stir into the cooked mushroom filling.

Fill the baked squash with leftover Bolognese, chilli or risotto, sprinkle with cheese and reheat as above.

Don't wash mushrooms as they absorb water like a sponge and then become tasteless. To clean, wipe with damp kitchen paper.

My Favourite Store Cupboard Chilli

I love this dish. It's so quick and easy to make, making it ideal for a speedy dinner. It also works well with overripe tomatoes. If you don't like your chilli too hot reduce the amount of chilli powder and cayenne pepper. If you like it super hot, try adding fresh red chillies.

Serves 4

3 onions, peeled and sliced

low calorie cooking spray

2 teaspoons ground cumin

4 teaspoons dried oregano

4 teaspoons paprika

½ teaspoon cayenne pepper

2 teaspoons chilli powder

4 cloves garlic, peeled and crushed

650g fresh tomatoes, chopped (canned would do too)

1 tablespoon red wine vinegar

2 cans black beans, rinsed and drained

salt and pepper

4 tablespoons fresh coriander leaves, chopped

Fry the onions in the low calorie cooking spray until softened and brown. Add the spices, garlic and tomatoes and cook for another 2-3 minutes. Add the vinegar and the beans. Cover and cook over a medium heat until the tomatoes have softened, the chilli has thickened slightly and is piping hot. If it starts to stick, add a little water.

Season with a little salt and pepper and serve sprinkled with the fresh coriander leaves.

Jayne's Tips

I love to serve this with rice, green pea guacamole (see recipe on p.58) and a huge green side salad.

If you have hungry mouths to feed, serve with warm crusty bread, wholemeal of course!

Creamy Potato and Spinach Curry

This is a delicious dish served as part of a curry or as a quick snack. I like to use silken tofu in this recipe because I find it doesn't curdle when heated, unlike the fat free/low fat yoghurts or fromage frais. You could use low fat yoghurt or fromage frais in this recipe but if you do warm very, very gently.

Serves 4

low calorie cooking spray

750g new potatoes, washed (no need to peel)

1 packet silken tofu

1 onion, peeled and finely chopped

2 cloves garlic, peeled and crushed

1 teaspoon black mustard seeds

½ teaspoon ground turmeric

½ teaspoon ground cumin

1 teaspoon ground coriander

1 teaspoon garam masala

salt and pepper

250g fresh spinach leaves, washed and drained

fresh mint leaves, chopped

extra black mustard seeds

Preheat the oven to 180C/Gas 4 and spray a baking tray with low calorie cooking spray.

Place the new potatoes onto the tray halving any that are large and spray well. Bake until cooked through, about 35-40 minutes.

Whilst the potatoes are cooking, blend the tofu with a stick blender or processor until smooth.

Fry the onion in a sprayed pan until golden brown and soft. Add the garlic and remaining spices and cook for another minute. Stir in the tofu sauce and cooked potatoes mixing everything together so the potatoes are coated. Heat gently for about 5 minutes, then season to taste with a little salt and pepper.

Just before serving turn off the heat and add the spinach leaves. There should be enough heat in the pan to wilt down the leaves but still leaving them with a little crunch. Serve sprinkled with chopped mint leaves and extra black mustard seeds scattered over the top.

Jayne's Tips

This recipe is great to use up any old potatoes you have
lying about in the kitchen cupboards.

My Amazing Spicy Bean and Butternut Tagine

This dish is not only colourful to look at, it's so simple to make. It's brilliant served for lunch or dinner, as a topping for jacket potatoes or even as an accompaniment to cooked meat or fish. Leftovers can be mixed into cooked pasta stretching it even further. The list goes on and on and I am sure you'll find countless other uses for it too.

Serves 4

1 onion, peeled and sliced

low calorie cooking spray

1 teaspoon cumin seeds

2 garlic cloves, peeled and crushed

1 butternut squash, seeded and cubed, no need to peel

2 sweet potatoes, scrubbed and cubed, no need to peel

2 peppers, seeds and pith removed, flesh chopped

1 red chilli, seeded and chopped

2 x 400g cans mixed beans

2 x 400g cans chopped tomatoes

2 teaspoons smoked/plain paprika

salt and pepper

small bunch coriander, chopped (optional)

Fry the onion in a large pan that's been sprayed with low calorie cooking spray until golden brown. Add the cumin seeds and crushed garlic and cook for a further minute. Next add the remaining ingredients with the exception of the salt and pepper and coriander. Bring to the boil, adding a cup of water or two if it looks dry. Cover the pan and simmer until the vegetables are cooked, about 20 minutes.

Season with a little salt and pepper and serve sprinkled with the coriander.

Chilli Bean Taco Wraps

You don't need to specifically make chilli for this recipe, leftover chilli works just as well. For example, leftover chilli from the Ragu recipe (see recipe on p.87) can be adapted by throwing in an extra can of beans, cooked peppers, leftover vegetables or adding a can of sweetcorn. If you want to be virtuous and avoid the high calorie tortilla wrap, why not use crispy iceberg lettuce leaves as a delicious alternative. An unusual but surprisingly, refreshing variation and very healthy too. However, if made this way they'll need to be eaten immediately, as the lettuce will begin to wilt. Alternatively use Taco shells. These are readily available from supermarkets, which is a half way compromise. But what the hell, if you're in a reckless mood, use a tortilla wrap!

Serves 4

1 onion, peeled and chopped

low calorie cooking spray

1 clove garlic, peeled and chopped

1 tablespoon ground cumin

3 peppers, chopped, seeds and pith removed

2 x 400g cans chilli beans (or use kidney beans and 1 can chopped tomatoes)

1 x 425g can sweetcorn, drained

1 can water/vegetable stock

large iceberg lettuce leaves/taco shells

fresh coriander leaves, chopped

Fry the onion in the low calorie cooking spray until soft, about 5 minutes. Then add the garlic and cumin and cook for a further minute. Next add the peppers and cook for another 2-3 minutes. Stir in the chilli beans, sweetcorn and one can of water. Cover the pan and simmer until the peppers are cooked and everything is piping hot, about 20 minutes.

For the lettuce wraps, select the largest leaves to form 4 wraps. You will need several leaves per wrap so there is some substance. Snapping each of the lettuce leaves at the stalk end will make the leaves flat and rolling easier.

Having prepared your lettuce wraps, divide the bean mixture between them, sprinkle over the chopped coriander and simply roll them up! Or just fill the taco shells, sprinkling the coriander on top. Serve by themselves or accompanied with potato wedges (see recipe on p.172) and salad.

Meltingly Soft Stuffed Aubergines

D E L I C I O U S! I can't describe this dish any other way. Aubergines are one of those vegetables that can be hit or miss. Personally I think it all depends upon the recipe. Yummy and meltingly soft this is brilliant as a main vegetarian dish, as a light lunch or vegetable accompaniment with meat or fish. Some people recommend salting aubergines to extract bitter flavours but personally I don't think it's necessary nowadays, but salt away if you feel the urge.

Serves 4

2 large aubergines, halved lengthways

low calorie cooking spray

1 onion, skinned and finely chopped

4-6 cloves garlic, peeled and finely chopped

3 tomatoes, chopped

small bunch parsley, finely chopped

small bunch dill, finely chopped

salt and pepper

1 tablespoon sweetener

water

lemon quarters

Place the halved aubergines cut side upwards, into a wide and heavy based pan that's been sprayed with low calorie cooking spray. Mix together the remaining ingredients except for the water and lemons and heap this onto the aubergine halves and spray thoroughly.

Drizzle enough water into the pan to cover the base. Cover and cook on a very low heat until the aubergines and filling are soft, about 1-2 hours. From time to time, lift the lid and gently press the filling down. Drizzle in extra water to prevent sticking.

The end result will be beautiful soft aubergines, full of flavour and a little sticky sauce at the bottom. Yum! No more words needed!

Serve these hot or leave to cool in the pan and serve at room temperature garnished with lemon quarters.

My Amazing Guilt Free Onion and Gruyere Quiche

I was really excited when I developed this recipe as I knew it would have a positive impact on my future eating habits. I couldn't wait to share it with others. I don't feel that I'm watching my weight when I eat this as it looks and tastes just like a real quiche. The best part though is that it's guilt free because I have replaced the pastry with a potato base.

Serves 6-8

FOR THE BASE

low calorie cooking spray

450g potatoes, washed and peeled

½ small onion, peeled

1 tablespoon Parmesan cheese, grated (optional)

salt and pepper

1 egg, beaten

FOR THE FILLING

500g onions, peeled and thinly sliced

150ml skimmed milk

4 eggs

180g Gruyere cheese, grated

Preheat the oven to 220C/Gas 7. Spray a 23cm solid based ovenproof dish with low calorie cooking spray and line the base with a circle of non-stick paper, spray again and set aside.

Stand a grater inside a large bowl and using the large holes, grate the potatoes followed by the onion. Stir in the Parmesan cheese, a little salt and pepper and the beaten egg. Then taking large handfuls of the mixture, squeeze out any excess liquid and transfer to the lined dish. Press down into the base and up the sides. Continue until you have completely lined the dish and spray. Then bake in the oven for 20 minutes. Spray again and return to the oven. Bake until the potato shell is crispy and golden brown, another 10-15 minutes. Leave to cool. Reduce the oven temperature to 190C/ Gas 5.

Prepare the filling by frying the onions over a low heat with the spray, until golden brown. Take your time, as you don't want them to burn.

Mix together the milk, eggs and a little salt and pepper.

Cover the baked potato shell with a thin layer of cheese and top with the onions, finishing with the remaining cheese. Place the dish onto a baking tray, pour in the milk and egg mixture and bake until firm and golden, about 30 minutes. Leave to stand for about 10 minutes to firm up.

Vegetarian

To unmould, run a small knife around the sides of the quiche. Place a tray or plate on top and flip over the dish and plate so that the quiche is now upside down. Remove the dish and peel off the non-stick paper (which is now facing upwards) and place a serving plate over the base and flip over again. Serve with a crisp green salad or vegetables in season.

Jayne's Tips

Cold quiche or any leftovers are great served as a portable lunch or a quick snack.

Stuffed Pancakes with Spinach and Ricotta

Pancakes can be used in so many ways. They are great served with lemon juice and sweetener (see recipe on p.28) or stuffed with leftover vegetables or Bolognese sauce for a speedy supper. They can be made in advance for a quick and easy meal plus any leftover pancakes can be frozen and used at a later date. In this recipe you can substitute the ricotta with low fat cottage cheese for a lower fat option or instead of the pancakes use shop bought tubes of dried cannelloni and a piping bag (see my tips below).

Serves 4

340g ricotta cheese, drained

400g fresh spinach, washed and drained

freshly grated nutmeg (to taste)

1 bunch spring onions, trimmed and finely sliced

salt and pepper

8 cooked pancakes (see recipe on p.28)

low calorie cooking spray

TOPPING

180g mozzarella cheese, grated

1 quantity white sauce, warmed (see recipe on p.177)

2 tablespoons Parmesan cheese, grated

Preheat the oven to 200C/Gas 6.

Place the drained ricotta cheese into a sieve and rub through using a wooden spoon or ladle. This gives the cheese a soft, smooth texture. Cook the spinach in a large pan until it wilts stirring frequently, about 1-2 minutes. Drain well and squeeze hard to remove any excess liquid until quite dry. Roughly chop and mix with the cheese, nutmeg, spring onions and a little salt and pepper.

To assemble, place the pancakes onto a work surface. Divide the filling equally between them placing the filling on a quarter segment of the pancake. Fold in half, enclosing the filling and then fold in half again. You should now have something that resembles a 'v' shape.

Transfer the folded pancakes into an ovenproof dish sprayed with low calorie cooking spray, top with grated mozzarella, cover with white sauce and sprinkle with Parmesan cheese. Bake until the top is brown and the sauce is bubbling, about 25-30 minutes. Serve with your choice of salads or vegetables.

Chick Pea and Broccoli Burgers

A delicious alternative to the classic beef burger. I simply love this served in a wholemeal bun with salad, crisp onion rings and drizzled with sweet chilli sauce, although ketchup is good too. If you are trying to introduce children to vegetables then this smuggles in a little broccoli – delicious!

Serves 4

200g purple sprouting broccoli, washed

1 tablespoon water

1 onion, peeled and finely chopped

low calorie cooking spray

2 garlic cloves, peeled and crushed

1 red chilli, finely chopped, seeds discarded

400g can chick peas, rinsed and drained

1 egg

small handful fresh coriander, chopped

120g Gruyere/Cheddar cheese, grated

1 lemon, zest grated

2 teaspoons ground coriander

salt and pepper

FOR SERVING

4 x 60g wholemeal rolls

lettuce leaves, tomato slices, red onion rings

sweet chilli sauce or sour cream/garlic dip (see recipes on p.61 and p.59)

Preheat the oven to 200C/Gas 6.

Trim the end off each broccoli stalk and place them into a microwavable dish with 1 tablespoon of water. Cover and cook in the microwave until tender, about 3-4 minutes. Leave to cool.

Fry the onion in the low calorie cooking spray until soft. Add the garlic and chilli and cook for a further minute. Place the cooked broccoli into a food processor with the remaining ingredients and pulse until you have a smoothish looking mixture. Don't take it as far as a puree, you need some texture left.

Divide into 4 burger shapes, place onto a sprayed baking tray and refrigerate for 30 minutes, if time allows, to firm up. Then bake until golden brown, about 20-25 minutes.

Serve your burger in the roll topped with the lettuce, tomato and red onion and sauce. You can accompany these burgers with spiced sweet potato wedges (see recipe on p.172).

Baked Gnocchi with Spinach and Mushrooms

Gnocchi are little potato and wheat dumplings which, once cooked, can be served either as a substitute for potatoes, rice or pasta. They are very versatile, so it's always worth having a packet to hand in the larder! Packets of dried gnocchi can be found alongside dried pasta in the supermarket.

Serves 4 as a filling main course

500g chestnut mushrooms, halved

low calorie cooking spray

2 cloves garlic, peeled and crushed

1kg dried gnocchi

400g baby spinach leaves

340g ricotta cheese or low fat cottage cheese

salt and pepper

freshly grated nutmeg (to taste)

Preheat the oven to 180C/Gas 4.

Fry the mushrooms in the low calorie cooking spray until golden brown, about 3-4 minutes. Then add the garlic and cook for a further minute. Set aside.

Meanwhile, bring a pan of salted water to the boil, add the gnocchi and cook for 3 minutes. As the gnocchi cook, they'll rise to the surface, at which point they can be removed with a slotted spoon and set aside in a bowl.

Place the spinach in a large pan, no need to add any water, and heat until wilted, stirring frequently. This should only take a few minutes. Turn off the heat and add the cooked mushrooms, ricotta, a little salt and pepper and nutmeg. Gently fold in the gnocchi, transfer to a sprayed ovenproof dish and bake until bubbling, about 20 minutes. Serve with a mixed salad.

Baked Pumpkin with Creamy Cheese Fondue

These little pumpkin shells are great filled with chilli, Bolognese, a dip or sauce. This recipe uses the pumpkin as a delicious container for a warm creamy cheese fondue, which could be served either on its own, or with vegetable crudities for a first course or supper. As an added bonus there's no washing-up - you can eat the entire thing.

Serves 4

low calorie cooking spray

4 baby pumpkins

FOR THE CREAMY CHEESE FONDUE

120g Gruyere cheese, grated

sour cream and chive dip (see recipe on p.59)

Preheat the oven to 190C/Gas 5 and spray a baking tray or dish large enough to accommodate the pumpkins with the low calorie cooking spray.

Carefully remove the top third of the pumpkins with a sharp knife. The easiest way I find to do this is by carefully scoring around its flesh, then working the knife gently through to remove the top. Scoop out the seeds and membrane with a teaspoon and discard, then replace the lids.

Place the pumpkins onto the tray, spraying well and bake until cooked, about 30-40 minutes. The easiest way to check they are cooked is by inserting a skewer through the flesh, which should easily pass through.

To turn this into a creamy cheese fondue, first divide half the grated cheese between the cooked pumpkins. Then top with the dip and sprinkle over the rest of the cheese. Replace the lids and bake until piping hot and the cheese has melted, about 5-10 minutes.

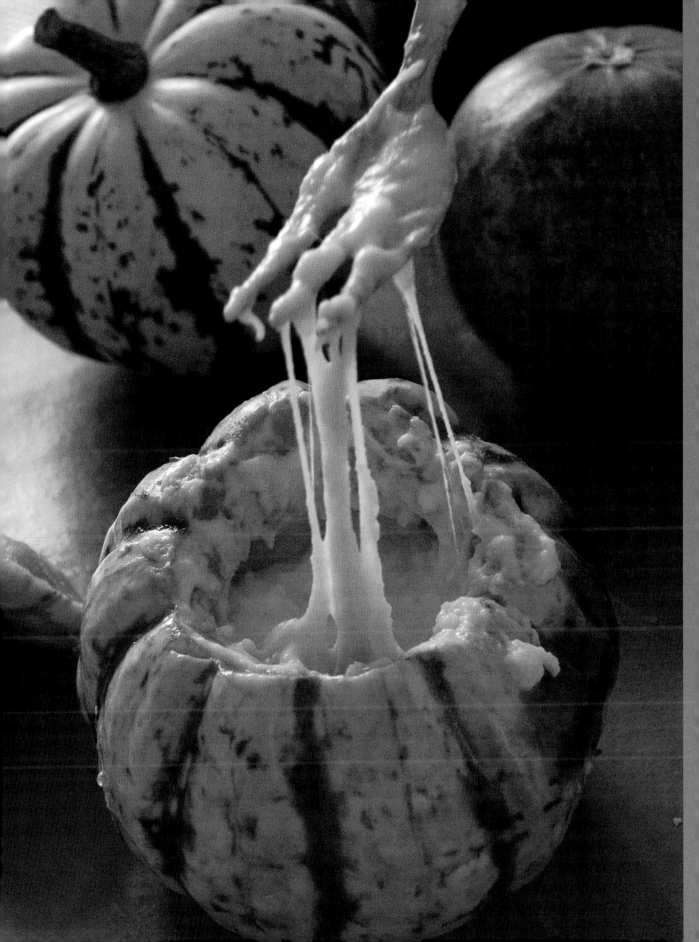

Butternut Squash to Die For!

An unusual vegetable dish that can be served either as an accompaniment to meat or fish, as a vegetarian main course, or simply on a bed of warmed couscous. I have even eaten leftovers cold, straight from the fridge! You might find those who dislike butternut squash, and I know one of those, actually quite like this dish. So here's hoping for other converts. A word about preparing squash – you don't need to peel it as the skin takes on a really soft texture once cooked, plus it contains fibre too. But peel away if you prefer.

The amount of oil in this recipe is minimal and when split between four equates to 1½ teaspoons each. However if you are short on time use shop bought pesto but be warned it will contain oil too.

Serves 4

FOR THE SPICE CRUST

1 tablespoon cumin seeds

½ tablespoon coriander seeds

¼ teaspoon ground allspice

1 tablespoon sumac powder or
1 teaspoons lemon zest

1 tablespoon mild paprika

1 bunch spring onions, washed, trimmed and chopped

1 butternut squash, washed

low calorie cooking spray

FOR THE CORIANDER AND GINGER PESTO

1 small piece ginger, about the size of your thumb, peeled and chopped

1 clove garlic, peeled and crushed

5 tablespoons fresh coriander, chopped

1 teaspoon sweetener

1 lemon, juiced and zest finely grated

2 tablespoons olive oil

salt and pepper

Preheat the oven to 200C/Gas 6.

Prepare the squash by cutting off the top and bottom. Cut in half lengthways and remove the seeds with a teaspoon. Cut each half into wedges, place into the bowl containing the spice crust and coat thoroughly.

Transfer the squash onto a baking tray that's been sprayed with low calorie cooking spray and sprinkle over any spice crust that was left behind. Spray everything well. Roast until slightly charred and tender, about 40-50 minutes.

Whilst the squash is cooking blend the pesto ingredients together. It's that quick!

Once the squash is cooked serve drizzled with the pesto adding a little salt and pepper if necessary.

Jayne's Tips

Use different herbs and spices to make up your own
flavoured pesto. Go on be adventurous!

Substitute the oil in the pesto for fat free vinaigrette.

Pasta and Rice

Spaghetti with Tomatoes, Chilli and Olives

The colours in this dish are so vibrant it just calls out 'eat me'! It's a perfect dish to serve when time is short or when you don't want to be slaving over a hot stove. Most of the ingredients will probably be in your larder anyway – an added bonus. You could use different types of pasta, canned tomatoes instead of fresh, change the herbs and omit the chilli if you wish. Whatever you do, make it your own and enjoy, it's quick and delicious so what more could you ask for especially after a hard days work!

Serves 4

300g dried spaghetti

1kg fresh tomatoes, chopped

low calorie cooking spray

1 red chilli, finely chopped, seeds discarded

8 anchovy fillets, rinsed, drained and chopped (optional)

3 cloves garlic, peeled and crushed

2 tablespoons capers, drained

32 black olives, drained and sliced

salt and pepper

small handful chopped fresh parsley

Bring a pan of lightly salted water to the boil, add the spaghetti and cook for 10-12 minutes or according to the packet instructions, then drain.

Whilst the spaghetti is cooking fry the tomatoes in the low calorie cooking spray until soft. Add the chilli, anchovy fillets and garlic and cook for a further minute. Next throw in the capers, black olives and pepper. Stir in the spaghetti mixing well and serve sprinkled with fresh parsley and accompanied by a side salad.

Jayne's Tips

Vegetarians can substitute a sheet of nori (seaweed) for the anchovies for that salty kick.

Quick and Easy Lasagne

My version of the traditional lasagne can be made with extra lean mince or vegetarian mince, both low in fat and equally delicious.

Serves 4

1 onion, peeled and chopped

1 carrot, peeled and chopped

low calorie cooking spray

2 cloves garlic, peeled and chopped

500g extra lean beef/lamb/vegetarian mince

400g can chopped tomatoes

500g carton passata

2 tablespoons tomato puree

salt and pepper

sweetener (optional)

9 sheets dried lasagne

1 quantity white sauce, warmed (see recipe on p.177)

120g Cheddar cheese, grated

Preheat the oven to 180C/Gas 4.

Prepare the meat sauce by frying the onion and carrot until soft and golden brown in a pan that's been sprayed with low calorie cooking spray. Add the garlic and cook for a further minute.

Next, add the mince and cook until slightly brown. Stir in the tomatoes, passata and tomato puree, cover with a lid and reduce the heat to medium-low. Simmer until the sauce has cooked and thickened, about 30-40 minutes. Season to taste with a little salt and pepper. If the sauce tastes a little bitter, add a pinch of sweetener - the sweetener is used to balance the acidity in the tomatoes.

To assemble, spray a 23cm square ovenproof dish and lay three lasagne sheets on the base. Cover with half the meat sauce followed by another layer of the lasagne sheets and top with the remaining sauce. Place the last three sheets on top, cover the surface with white sauce and sprinkle over the grated cheese. Cover at this stage and refrigerate overnight if you're preparing ahead of time.

Place on a baking tray and bake until bubbling and golden, about 40 minutes. If cooking straight from the refrigerator add a further 10 minutes to the cooking time.

Serve with a salad of your choice.

Macaroni Cheese with Caramelised Onions

Who doesn't like macaroni cheese? Traditional recipes use butter, milk, cheese and sometimes cream, all laden with fat. This version is not only lighter on the fat but it also includes caramelised onions which take it to another level, making a beautiful, creamy and delicious combination.

Serves 4

2 medium onions, peeled and thinly sliced

low calorie cooking spray

1 tablespoon balsamic vinegar

400g macaroni pasta shapes

1 quantity white sauce (see recipe on p.177)

180g reduced fat cheddar cheese, coarsely grated

salt and pepper

extra balsamic vinegar to drizzle (optional)

extra grated cheese for serving (optional)

First cook the onions. The best way to caramelise them is to fry them over a low heat in a covered, non-stick frying pan that's been sprayed with low calorie cooking spray. Stir from time to time adding more spray if the onions start to stick. Don't rush this process because you want them meltingly soft and not burnt to a crisp that will taste bitter! The whole process could take up to 20-30 minutes. Then stir in the balsamic vinegar and cook for a further minute until absorbed.

To cook the macaroni bring a large saucepan of lightly salted water to the boil. Add the pasta, reduce the heat to medium and cook until tender, about 12 minutes or according to packet instructions. Drain.

To assemble, reheat the white sauce until piping hot. Add the cheese and macaroni, stirring well. Season with a little salt and pepper. Next, gently fold in the onions until you end up with a rippled effect that has patches of macaroni cheese studded with pockets of caramelised onions.

Serve drizzled with extra balsamic vinegar and topped with a little grated cheese. Steamed snow peas and a beetroot and pear salad make a great accompaniment (see recipe on p.151) to this dish.

Jayne's Tips

To make this extra cheesy you could add more cheese
to the recipe but bear in mind the extra energy intake.

Before serving you could also sprinkle the top with extra
cheese and flash under the grill for a few minutes for a
crispy golden topping.

You could substitute the onions for mushrooms or use
caramelised red onions instead of white ones to make
different variations.

The 'Bees Knees' Roasted Tomato and Pesto Lasagne

If I had a favourite lasagne, this would be it! Believe me this is so good the carnivores in the family won't notice the absence of meat. In fact I'm sure this will become a firm family favourite - it is with mine. For variety, use different coloured tomatoes. Leftovers, if there are any, can be eaten cold for a speedy snack or easily reheated. What better than to have something healthy and delicious on standby!

Serves 4

low calorie cooking spray

1 quantity basic white sauce, warmed (see recipe on p.177)

9-10 dried lasagne sheets

4 tablespoons red pesto, or more if required

600g fresh cherry tomatoes, washed and halved

1 packet fresh basil leaves

salt and pepper

260g reduced fat mozzarella cheese, grated

Preheat the oven to 180C/Gas 4 and spray a 23cm square, ovenproof dish with low calorie cooking spray.

The completed lasagne comprises 2 layers of filling sandwiched between 3 layers of lasagne sheets. To assemble the lasagne, drizzle a little of the white sauce over the base of the dish. Layer lasagne sheets, pre-spread with a little red pesto, over the white sauce, breaking them to fit as necessary. Scatter half the tomatoes on top, torn basil leaves and a little salt and pepper. Then sprinkle with one-third of the grated mozzarella cheese and drizzle with a little white sauce. Repeat these steps once more. The final layer of lasagne should be placed pesto-side down and then covered with the remaining white sauce and grated cheese.

This is now ready to be baked or can be covered and refrigerated overnight if preparing ahead of time.

To cook, place on a baking tray and bake until bubbling and the cheese is golden brown, approximately 30–40 minutes. Allow an extra 5-10 minutes cooking time if the dish comes straight from the refrigerator.

Serve with your favourite salad and crusty wholemeal bread for those hungriest of eaters.

Jayne's Tips

Pre-cooked lasagne sheets can be used straight from
the packet but if time allows I prefer to cook the sheets
first. This gives a better texture and makes it easier to
cut and shape them using scissors when assembling. But
of course this is optional. Drop separated sheets into
boiling water until softened (5 minutes or so). Drain
under cold running water, then separate the sheets and
cut to fit your dish.

Butternut Squash Risotto

I love risotto. It's so comforting and delicious to eat. This version takes slightly longer to make than a normal risotto but it's really worth the extra time. To reduce the preparation and cooking time prepare the mashed squash the day before and chill until needed. I have to say that my son dislikes squash with a vengeance but will happily plough his way through this risotto. Don't forget you can change the flavour by using all sorts of vegetable combinations.

This is delicious served as a starter or as a main course accompanied with a crisp green salad. If you want to transform it into a showstopper, maybe for a special meal or just to impress, why not garnish it with a Parmesan Crisp (see recipe on p.57). They are much easier than they look!

Serves 4

1 butternut squash, washed

1 onion, peeled and finely chopped

1 shallot, peeled and finely chopped

low calorie cooking spray

2 cloves garlic, peeled and finely chopped

150ml water

salt and pepper

300g arborio risotto rice

1 litre vegetable stock

1½ teaspoons fresh ginger, grated

balsamic vinegar (optional)

1 tablespoon fresh parsley, chopped

4 tablespoons Parmesan cheese, grated

Preheat the oven to 180C/Gas 4.

Prepare the butternut squash by cutting off the top and bottom. Cut in half lengthways and remove the seeds with a teaspoon. Take one half of the squash and remove the skin with a vegetable peeler. I find the wide swivel type peeler best for this job. Then cut into 2.5cm cubes and set aside.

Next, cook the onion and shallot in a pan that's been sprayed with low calorie cooking spray until softened. Whilst this is cooking, prepare the other half of the squash by slicing it into wedges and placing onto a sprayed baking tray (no need to peel). Roast in the oven until slightly charred around the edges, about 40-50 minutes, then cover with foil to keep warm.

When the onion and shallots are cooked, add the garlic and cook for a further minute. Once this stage is reached, place half of this mixture into a bowl, saving for later, leaving the other half in the pan.

Add the cubed squash pieces and 150ml of water to the half that's in the pan. Cover and simmer until soft, about 15 minutes. Once cooked, mash the contents with a fork or masher and season to taste with a little salt and pepper. Set aside until needed.

To make the risotto, put the reserved onion and garlic mixture into a deep-sided frying pan, add the rice and over a low heat cook until the risotto rice is slightly transparent. Add the stock, a little at a time and cook until each addition has been absorbed, this will take about 30 minutes. Remember stir from time to time to prevent it sticking to the bottom of the pan. Stir in the reserved mashed squash, ginger and balsamic vinegar and heat.

Serve, topped with the roasted wedges and sprinkled with fresh parsley and grated cheese.

My All Purpose Pasta Pie

This recipe consists of two dishes in one, and when you're short of time I think dishes like this are so handy. There are so many ways to vary the fillings - think of your own favourite savoury tart or quiche and then substitute the ingredients.

The main component in this dish is orzo pasta. Don't be fooled into thinking it's rice by its appearance – it looks like a rice grain but it's actually pasta, a brilliant ingredient and cheap too! I use an ovenproof pan that's suitable for cooking on the stove as well as in the oven. If you don't have one, use an ordinary frying pan and then transfer the mixture into an ovenproof dish.

Serves 6 large portions

6 assorted coloured peppers, cut into strips, seeds and pith removed

6 garlic cloves, unpeeled low calorie cooking spray

1 large onion, peeled and finely chopped

500g orzo pasta

1 litre vegetable stock

180g Cheddar cheese, grated

salt and pepper

Preheat the oven to 180C/Gas 4.

Place the pepper strips and garlic cloves onto a large baking tray that's been sprayed with low calorie cooking spray and bake until soft, about 30 minutes. Leave to cool. Then increase the oven temperature to 240C/Gas 8-9.

In a frying pan fry the onion in the spray until golden brown. Stir in the orzo pasta, vegetable stock, three-quarters of the cheese and half the cooked pepper strips and season to taste with a little salt and pepper. Squeeze the flesh from the garlic skins and stir into the mixture. Top with the remaining peppers arranging them evenly and bring the whole dish up to a gentle boil. Turn off the heat, sprinkle with the remaining cheese and bake in the oven until cooked and golden brown, about 20 minutes.

Serve with a Bonjuk Salad (see recipe on p.154) or grilled asparagus, baby corn or vegetables of your choice.

Quick and Easy Roasted Pepper Lasagne

As the recipe title suggests this dish is super quick to prepare especially if you have a jar of roasted peppers in your larder. The instructions for both the jarred and fresh peppers are included.

I never remove the skins from fresh roasted peppers - why throw away added fibre. I'm a firm believer that you eat with your eyes first and if it looks good you're half way there – especially with children, so use a variety of colours to add that eye-catching appeal.

Serves 4

9 peppers, assorted in colour or 2-3 jars roasted peppers in brine

low calorie cooking spray

2 x 500g cartons passata

250g dried lasagne sheets

120g Gruyere or Cheddar cheese, grated

salt and pepper

FOR THE TOPPING

1 x quantity white sauce, warmed (see recipe on p.177)

Preheat the oven to 180C/Gas 4.

To prepare the fresh peppers, first cut off their tops, discarding the stalk and slice the flesh. Cut off the sides and bottoms of the peppers, discarding any seeds and white membrane, then cut each pepper piece into strips or wedges and place onto a baking tray that's been sprayed with low calorie cooking spray and spray again. Roast until soft, about 25-30 minutes and leave to cool (this stage can be prepared the day before).

If using the jarred variety all you need to do is rinse and drain the peppers and cut into strips or wedges.

The completed lasagne comprises 3 layers of filling sandwiched between 4 layers of lasagne sheets. To assemble, spray a 23cm square, ovenproof dish, drizzle the bottom with a little passata and place a layer of lasagne sheets on top (you may need to snap some of the sheets in order to make them fit so they don't overlap). Drizzle over more passata ensuring the sheets are coated then add a layer of the peppers. Season with a little salt and pepper and sprinkle over one quarter of the grated cheese and a drizzle of passata. This creates one layer.

Repeat this process to create a further two layers. Finish with a final layer of lasagne sheets. Pour over the white sauce and sprinkle with the remaining cheese.

If preparing in advance you can now cover the dish and refrigerate.

Bake until piping hot and golden, about 30-40 minutes. Allow an extra 10 minutes cooking time if the dish comes straight from the refrigerator.

I like to serve this dish with a roasted red onion and watercress salad (see recipe on p.155).

Jayne's Tips

If you're serving this with the roasted red onion and watercress salad, to save time you could roast the red onions with the peppers.

Pre-cooked lasagne sheets can be used straight from the packet but if time allows I prefer to cook them first. This gives a better texture to the finished dish and makes it easier to cut and shape when layering. Drop each sheet separately into boiling water and cook until softened (5 minutes or so). Drain under cold running water, then separate to prevent them sticking together.

Salads and Vegetables

Beetroot and Pear Salad

An amazing salad, not only in flavour but colour too. It simply oozes health and tastes absolutely fantastic. It's packed full of vitamins, (don't tell the kids!) and large amounts of fibre as well. Eat as an accompaniment to meat, fish and vegetarian dishes. I simply love eating it as a snack, straight from the fridge. Vary by adding chopped parsley, coriander, chives, or anything else you have available, or substitute the fruit for grated carrot. There are so many possibilities I could go on forever.

Serves 1 to 4 depending upon appetite

1 large raw beetroot, washed

1-2 pears depending on their size, unpeeled

Cut off the top and root from the beetroot and then remove its peel. Stand a grater inside a large bowl and using the large hole, grate the beetroot followed by the pears.

Once grated, simply mix both together and there you have it, it's that easy.

Chill in the fridge until required (if you can wait that long!).

Jayne's Tips

Use disposable gloves to avoid red hands!

Substitute the pears for apples as an alternative.

Mixed Bean Salad

You don't need to be a vegetarian to enjoy beans. This dish adds variety to every day salads with the bonus of including extra protein and fibre too. Eat on its own as a healthy snack or serve alongside grilled fish or meat. It's so quick to put together and can be varied using any canned beans.

Serves 6

FOR THE DRESSING

2 tablespoons fat free vinaigrette dressing

I clove garlic, peeled and crushed

½ teaspoon Dijon mustard

salt and pepper

FOR THE SALAD

I can kidney beans, rinsed and drained

I can chick peas, rinsed and drained

I can butter beans, rinsed and drained

I small onion, peeled and chopped

Place all the dressing ingredients together in an empty jam jar, screw on the lid and shake.

Combine the beans, chick peas and onion in a large bowl then pour over the dressing, mixing together. Cover and refrigerate until needed.

Couscous with Chilli and Mango

If you're really hungry this dish can be made in a matter of minutes (the time it takes for the couscous to absorb the boiling water). Serve on its own for a light lunch, as an alternative to potatoes, rice or pasta to a main meal or even use for a packed lunch or picnic. It's so adaptable, so have a go! Substitute your own favourite fruit and spices and if you want to introduce variety or make it more substantial add cooked chicken, prawns, chick peas, or leftovers - the limit is your imagination.

Serves 4

200g dried couscous

zest 2 lemons, finely grated

1-2 mangos, peeled, flesh chopped

small bunch fresh coriander, washed and chopped

chilli flakes (to taste)

salt and pepper

Place the couscous in a large bowl and pour over enough boiling water to just cover. Cover the bowl with a plate or cling film and leave to stand for approximately 5 minutes whilst you prepare the lemons, mangos, chop the coriander and hunt out the chilli flakes and a little salt and pepper from the cupboard. Then fluff up the couscous with a fork and fold in the remaining ingredients. Serve or cover and refrigerate until needed.

My Version of Bonjuk Salad

Jayne's Tips

This is great served with grilled meat or fish, as part of a BBQ, eaten on its own as a snack or for a refreshing lunch.

On a family holiday to Turkey we dined at a restaurant that served this wonderful salad. It was so delicious I plucked up the courage to ask for the recipe but unfortunately I was told it was a secret. So this is my version, minus the copious amounts of oil that accompanied the original one.

Serves 6 as a side salad

5 tomatoes, chopped

100g sultanas (optional)

2 carrots, peeled and grated

½ small red cabbage, shredded

1 packet rocket salad

FOR THE DRESSING

5 tablespoons fat free viniagrette

1 teaspoon Dijon mustard

2 garlic cloves, peeled and crushed

salt and pepper

Mix together the tomatoes, sultanas, carrots and red cabbage in a large bowl. Then mix all the dressing ingredients together (I find a jam jar really good for this task) and pour over the salad and combine.

If you want to serve this now mix in the rocket salad. Otherwise cover the bowl and refrigerate until ready to serve adding the rocket just before serving.

Roasted Red Onion and Watercress Salad

A delicious salad eaten as an accompaniment with meat or fish, or for a light lunch with the addition of a little feta or goats' cheese. Personally I like this straight from the oven although it's equally delicious served at room temperature.

Serves 4

500g red onions, skins removed and ends trimmed

low calorie cooking spray

2 tablespoons balsamic vinegar

1 tablespoon honey

1 dried red chilli, broken into pieces or dried chilli flakes

1 cinnamon stick

salt and pepper

150ml water

85g packet watercress, washed

FOR THE DRESSING

1 teaspoon honey

1 tablespoon balsamic vinegar

Preheat the oven to 220C/Gas 7.

Cut the onions into wedges (6 or 8 wedges depending on their size) and place onto a roasting tray that's been sprayed with low calorie cooking spray.

Mix together the balsamic vinegar, honey and chilli and pour over the onions, also adding the cinnamon stick, a little salt and pepper and 150ml of water. Roast uncovered. Stir after 20 minutes and continue cooking until the onions are really tender, another 25-30 minutes, by which time the liquid will have reduced to a thin coating on the base of the tray.

Transfer the onions onto a serving plate that's been lined with the watercress leaving the onion juices in the roasting tray. To the tray add the remaining honey and balsamic vinegar, 2 tablespoons of water, a little salt and pepper and stir well. Spoon over the salad and serve.

HOMEMADE CROUTONS

To add a crunch to this salad, serve with homemade croutons. To make these, cut some bread (preferably from a stale wholemeal loaf) into cubes. Tip them onto a sprayed baking tray, spray again and bake in a preheated oven, 180C/Gas 4, until golden brown. Keep an eye on them, turning frequently because once they start to brown they can quickly burn. Sprinkle over the assembled salad.

Jayne's Tips

Prepare the croutons at the same time as the onions but keep a very close watch on them as the oven temperature is hotter.

Moroccan Couscous

In my opinion couscous is one of those store cupboard staples you just can't do without. It's so versatile and quick to use, you could rustle up a meal in next to no time. It can be served both hot or cold, sweet or savoury, added to leftovers, an alternative to rice, pasta or potatoes or used as a filling. It's also great on a picnic or as a packed lunch. So many choices!

Ras el hanout is a Moroccan spice that can be found in supermarkets. Substitute it with ground cumin or coriander if you can't get hold of it.

Serves 4

200g couscous

½-1 teaspoon ras el hanout spicy paste

2 oranges, zest finely grated, flesh chopped

400g can chick peas, drained and rinsed

1 mango, peeled, chopped into small chunks

2 fresh peaches or nectarines, chopped

50g dried cranberries (optional)

salt and pepper

Place the couscous into a large bowl adding the ras el hanout and enough boiling water to just cover the couscous, cover the bowl with cling film and leave it to stand.

Once the water has been absorbed, fluff it up with a fork, distributing the spicy paste.

Add the remaining ingredients mixing well. Season with a little salt and pepper and serve dolloped with sweet chilli dip (see recipe), accompanied with a large green salad and grilled meat, chicken or fish.

To serve cold, leave to cool, cover and refrigerate until needed.

Noodles with Fresh Coriander Pesto

Noodles, who doesn't love them? This variation can be served simply on its own or as an accompaniment. Served cold it's great on a picnic, as a lunch for work or part of a buffet. Vary the ingredients with whatever you have in your fridge.

Serves 4

350g dried noodles

200g mangetout, trimmed and halved diagonally

fresh coriander leaves, chopped

FOR THE PESTO

8cm piece fresh ginger, peeled and roughly chopped

4 garlic cloves, peeled and crushed

4 red chillies, chopped, seeds discarded

large handful fresh coriander leaves

4 limes, juiced and zest finely grated

8 teaspoons dark soy sauce

pinch of sweetener (optional)

Cook the noodles according to the packet instructions adding the mangetout two minutes before the end of cooking. Drain and return to the pan.

Prepare the pesto by placing all the ingredients into a blender and blitz until a thick paste is formed. Add to the pan.

Warm the noodles for a minute or two mixing well until piping hot. Sprinkle with coriander leaves and serve.

(See photograph on p.78 Spicy Fish Parcels)

Jayne's Tips

For extra crunch add 100g beansprouts to the cooked noodles and mix with the pesto dressing.

Sweet and Sour Courgettes

Courgettes are very versatile. They can be stuffed, steamed, stir-fried, boiled, grated and used as a salad ingredient. For me, this transports the humble courgette to a different dimension. Serve as an accompaniment to meat, fish or vegetarian dishes, on its own for a snack or used as part of a meze plate.

Serves 4

500g courgettes, ends removed, cut into batons

low calorie cooking spray

1 onion, peeled and thinly sliced

2 garlic cloves, peeled and crushed

3 tablespoons tomato puree

2 sticks celery, chopped

32 black olives (more if required)

3 tablespoons red wine vinegar

25g raisins or sultanas (optional)

4 tablespoons sweetener (to taste)

1 tablespoon freshly chopped mint

salt and pepper

Fry the courgettes in batches in a pan that's been sprayed with low calorie cooking spray until starting to brown. Transfer to a plate and set aside.

Fry the onion until golden. Add the garlic and cook for a further 2 minutes. Add the tomato puree and celery, cover the pan and leave to cook for 5 minutes, stirring occasionally.

Add the black olives, red wine vinegar, raisins and sweetener, lower the heat and cook covered for a further 10 minutes adding a little water if it begins to stick or looks dry. Return the courgettes to the pan and cook for an additional 5 minutes. Add a little salt and pepper, turn off the heat and serve at room temperature sprinkled with mint.

Thai Noodle Salad

Do you love noodles? If so you're going to love these. They're not only delicious, filling and quick to make but can be varied in many ways. They're great as a cold snack or leftovers can quickly be microwaved. Noodles are one of those store cupboard staples worth having, especially rice noodles as they only take 3 minutes to cook. Serve straight up drizzled with sweet chilli sauce for those ravenous moments! Substitute any vegetables you have and adapt the dressing – it's totally up to you. The main thing is to enjoy cooking so try out new ideas. You may just stumble onto something amazing – if you do I want to be the first to know!

Serves 2

FOR THE NOODLES

low calorie cooking spray

1 bunch asparagus, stalk end removed, stems cut into 3 cm lengths

500g cherry tomatoes

250g shiitake mushrooms, thickly sliced (or substitute for chestnut mushrooms)

200g dried noodles

FOR THE DRESSING

5cm piece fresh root ginger, peeled and finely grated

5cm piece lemon grass, trimmed and finely shredded

1 garlic clove, peeled and crushed

1 tablespoon rice vinegar or white wine vinegar/sherry vinegar

1 teaspoon sweetener

3 tablespoons light soy sauce

1 tablespoon sweet chilli sauce

3 tablespoons chopped fresh coriander leaves

Preheat the oven to 200C/Gas 6.

Place the asparagus, tomatoes and mushrooms onto a baking tray that's been sprayed with low calorie cooking spray and spray again. Roast until tender, about 20 minutes.

Prepare the dressing by mixing all the ingredients together except the fresh coriander.

Cook the noodles according to the packet instructions, drain and tip back into the pan pouring over a little of the dressing and mix to coat. Serve the noodles topped with the roasted vegetables, drizzled with the remaining dressing and scattered with coriander.

Jayne's Tips

I like to serve this as a hot dish but it's equally good served cold.

Roasted Beetroot Salad

Roasted beetroot is completely different from the pickled jarred variety and can be treated as a salad ingredient or vegetable. Turn this salad into a main course by adding goat's cheese or another soft cheese.

Serves 4

4 raw beetroot, washed and topped and tailed

salt and pepper

1 tablespoon water

mixed salad leaves

balsamic vinegar

Preheat the oven to 180C/Gas 4.

Take a large sheet of foil and lay it onto your worktop. Place the prepared beetroot into the centre and season with a little salt and pepper. Gather up the sides of the foil, adding a tablespoon of water to moisten and fold the edges together to form a parcel.

Place onto a baking tray and roast for 1-2 hours. Cooking time will depend upon the size of the beetroot. When cooked the beetroot skin will come away easily when pressed with your fingers. (Be careful not to burn yourself). Leave to cool and then peel.

Slice into wedges and toss with mixed salad leaves, drizzled with a little balsamic vinegar.

Jayne's Tips

If time is short buy vacuum packed cooked beetroot
found in the chiller cabinet.

Citrus Salad

A delicious, light and refreshing salad, which can be served on its own or as an accompaniment to a lunch or evening meal. Try it, it's quite a surprise.

Serves 4

2 pink grapefruits

2 large oranges

8 radishes, topped and tailed and thinly sliced

1 packet pea shoots, rocket, watercress or salad leaves

salt and pepper

Remove the skin and pith from the fruit with a knife (see Jayne's Tips below) and cut into thin slices.

Scatter the green leaves over a serving plate, placing the fruit slices alternatively on top followed by the radishes. Sprinkle with a little salt and pepper and serve.

Jayne's Tips

Pith or skin not removed can give the salad a bitter taste, which is why a knife is used to ensure a thorough job.

Rice and Courgette Salad

This combination came to me when considering how to use up some leftover rice and my courgette and mustard relish recipe. The result is a salad with a subtle flavour that will compliment stronger tasting foods or just eaten as a snack.

For each mould you will need

4 heaped tablespoons cooked rice

2 tablespoons courgette and mustard relish (see recipe on p.55)

2 teaspoons mango chutney

Mix all the ingredients together in a bowl. To serve mound onto a serving plate. For a more professional look, pack into a ring mould, small bowl etc. and place onto a plate and chill. When ready to serve run a pallet knife around the inside edge of the mould and lift off leaving a neat, compact shape to impress your guests.

Jayne's Tips

I use a small empty can from baked beans as a ring mould. Cut the bottom off an empty tin so that you're left with a ring. Simple, cheap and environmental friendly!

Fresh Figs with Goats' Cheese

The best figs I have ever tasted are those from a Turkish market, the skins bursting with flavour and juiciness. Simply divine! This dish combines the sweet fruity flavour of the figs and the sweet/sour taste of the balsamic vinegar with the salty Parma ham, the peppery rocket and the creaminess of the goats' cheese to make a wonderful combination. Once you've tasted this you won't believe that something so delicious could be so easy to prepare. Have a go, you're in for a treat.

Serves 4

1 packet rocket

4 large ripe fresh figs, washed

30g Parma ham, (optional) all fat removed

4 x 35g soft goats' cheese

balsamic vinegar

salt and pepper

Divide the rocket between plates. Then take a sharp knife and make two incisions about three-quarters of the way down each fig to form a cross. Be careful not to cut all the way through! Pinch the sides at the base and push so they open. Wrap the Parma ham strips lightly around the base of each fig. Once prepared, place in the centre of the rocket-lined plate.

Next, lightly crumble over the goats' cheese and simply drizzle with balsamic vinegar. Season with a little salt and pepper.

Jayne's Tips

It's worth buying the best balsamic vinegar you can for this dish.

Substitute the goats' cheese with 4 x 45g of mozzarella and freshly ripened peaches or nectarines instead of the fresh figs.

For a more rustic look use 2 figs and cut into pieces placing them onto the rocket. Randomly lay the Parma ham over the top, crumble over the goats' cheese and drizzle with the vinegar. Season with a little salt and pepper and serve.

This looks great on a large platter for a buffet or as a first course.

Bean and Quinoa Salad

Quinoa is one of the unsung heroes of the grain family. Nutritionally it has a high protein content that makes it really beneficial for your health. Unfortunately it's not well known. It can have a slightly bitter taste however, which can be rectified by rinsing thoroughly under cold running water before cooking. The addition of herbs or spices makes it a tasty alternative to rice or pasta or used in salads as I have done here. It can also be used to make porridge for breakfast (see recipe on p.25).

Serves 4

FOR THE DRESSING

1 lime, juiced and zest finely grated

1 tablespoon sweetener

4 teaspoons Dijon mustard

salt and pepper

2 cloves garlic, peeled and crushed

FOR THE SALAD

2 cups frozen soya beans or broad beans

1 cup Quinoa, rinsed

1 red and 1 yellow pepper, diced, seeds discarded

½ red onion, peeled and finely chopped

small bunch coriander, chopped

Place all the ingredients for the dressing into a jar, cover with a lid and shake to combine. Set aside.

For the salad, microwave the beans according to the packet instructions, or place them in a pan of boiling water, cover and simmer for 3-4 minutes, then drain.

In a separate saucepan, bring 2 cups of water to the boil. Add the Quinoa, bring back to the boil, lower the heat, cover the pan and simmer until the water has been absorbed, about 10 minutes. Then, switch off the heat and let stand for 5 minutes. Transfer to a bowl and leave to cool.

Whilst the Quinoa is cooling combine the peppers, onion, coriander and beans in a bowl, mixing well.

To assemble, tip the Quinoa into the mixed pepper combination, add the dressing and toss. Cover the bowl and refrigerate for at least 30 minutes before serving.

Ruby Red Cabbage and Apple

Red cabbage generally makes an appearance once a year on the Christmas table. It's such a shame as it's a really delicious vegetable and in need of a revival.

Serves 4

750g approximately red cabbage

240g onions, peeled and thinly sliced

240g cooking apples, peeled, cored and roughly chopped

1 clove garlic, peeled and crushed

¼ teaspoon grated nutmeg

¼ teaspoon ground cinnamon

¼ teaspoon ground allspice

3 tablespoons sweetener

3 tablespoons red wine vinegar

salt and pepper

Prepare the cabbage by removing the outer leaves and discard. Cut into quarters including its white core, this part contains many nutrients. Then finely slice and place into a large saucepan.

Add the remaining ingredients and cover the surface with a circle of greaseproof paper to retain the moisture and flavour. Cover the pan and cook over a low heat until soft, about 2 hours. Check after an hour or so adding a little water if the mixture appears dry.

Once cooked serve immediately or cool and transfer into freezer boxes and freeze until required.

Sweet Potato Wedges

I just adore potato wedges. This recipe uses sweet potatoes, which are just as good. Serve them with the Sour Cream and Chive dip (see recipe on p.59), tomato ketchup or a salsa for a delicious and filling snack. 'Season-All' is a spice, readily available in supermarkets but can be substituted for cajun' or 'jerk' seasoning.

Serves 4

low calorie cooking spray

4 sweet potatoes, washed and scrubbed (no need to peel)

'season-all' seasoning (to taste)

Preheat the oven to 220C/Gas 7 and spray a large baking tray with low calorie cooking spray.

Cut the sweet potatoes into wedges and place onto the tray. Spray them and sprinkle over the seasoning. Bake until soft, golden and silently charred, about 25-30 minutes.

Jayne's Tips

For a special treat once the wedges are cooked, sprinkle with grated cheese and bake for another 1-2 minutes until melted. Yum!

Substitute old potatoes instead of the sweet variety. Par-boil these first, by placing them in a pan of boiling water, bring back to the boil and cook, until a knife just pierces through the flesh, about 6 minutes, then drain and continue as above.

Gratin Dauphinoise

If you've ever eaten Gratin Dauphinoise then you'll know what I'm going to say next. It's so unctuous (sums it up for me), it can be eaten straight from the bowl. (Hands up, it has been done!) However, the traditional version is cooked and layered with butter and double cream that will not only stick to your ribs but will clog your arteries as well. My version is full of flavour and light in consistency that won't have you reaching for a blood pressure monitor, although you may be reaching for second helpings

Serves 4 as part of a meal

1.2 kg potatoes such as King Edwards, Desiree

1-2 large cloves garlic, peeled and crushed

450ml skimmed milk

salt and pepper

freshly grated nutmeg (to taste)

low calorie cooking spray, butter flavour

Preheat the oven to 180C/Gas 4.

Peel and thinly slice the potatoes, place in a saucepan with the garlic, milk and a little salt and pepper and bring to the boil. Cover and simmer very gently until the potatoes are just tender, about 10 minutes. Gently stir to avoid the potatoes catching on the bottom of the pan.

Layer the potatoes in an ovenproof dish using the best slices for the top. Pour in the liquid from the saucepan and sprinkle with nutmeg.

Spray the top with low calorie cooking spray. Place the dish onto a baking tray and bake until bubbling and golden brown on top, about 30-40 minutes.

Sauces

White Sauce Two Ways

A white sauce is such a versatile component to many dishes but can be quite high in fat and therefore calories. I have included two recipes; one that uses sauce flour, the other using silken tofu. Many people have this misconception that soya products, like silken tofu, are ingredients used solely by veggies and vegans as an alternative source of protein. This is true but believe me silken tofu is a very versatile and useful ingredient and should be used by all. It contains protein and is low in calories and healthy too. It does however require the addition of herbs, spices and flavours to make it exciting to eat. Try it, as it might become a firm favourite and a much-used ingredient in many of your dishes.

These sauces can be used as you would a normal white sauce; spread on top of a lasagne or with the addition of cheese used as a coating for macaroni or cauliflower.

WHITE SAUCE NO. 1

Serves 4

1 packet silken tofu

120ml skimmed milk

1 teaspoon Dijon mustard

salt and pepper

Drain any liquid from the silken tofu and place in a food processor with the milk, mustard and blitz until smooth. If you don't have a food processor, place the ingredients into a jug and blend with a stick blender, or just whisk really hard in a bowl until all the lumps disappear. Transfer to a pan and heat until hot. Season to taste with a little salt and pepper. This is now ready to use.

WHITE SAUCE NO. 2

Serves 4

50g Carrs sauce flour

500ml skimmed milk

1 teaspoon Dijon mustard

salt and pepper

Place the sauce flour, milk and mustard into a saucepan and over a medium heat continuously whisk together to produce a very smooth, hot, silky sauce, which will take about 3 minutes. Season to taste with a little salt and pepper. This is now ready to use.

Mushroom Sauce

Sauces are great and can transform dishes from the plain to the extraordinary. Serve this sauce as an accompaniment to grilled steaks or chicken, over a jacket potato, or used as a filling or topping in vegetarian dishes. Add some exotic mushrooms for a special dinner.

Serves 4

low calorie cooking spray

1 onion, peeled and finely chopped

1 clove garlic, peeled and crushed

250g mushrooms, wiped clean and sliced

1 packet silken tofu

4 teaspoons Dijon mustard

60ml vegetable stock/water

salt and pepper

Fry the onion in the low calorie cooking spray until golden brown. Add the garlic and cook for a further minute. Add the sliced mushrooms and fry until all the liquid has evaporated.

Whilst the mushrooms are cooking prepare the sauce by placing the silken tofu, mustard and stock into a blender and blitz until smooth. Season with a little salt and pepper and add to the mushrooms. Stir well and cook until hot.

Jayne's Tips

For a more intense mushroom flavour, soak 30g dried mushrooms in boiling water until softened. Strain the liquid using it for part of the stock. Chop the mushroom flesh and fry it with the sliced mushrooms, proceed as above.

Substitute the stock with skimmed milk for a creamier mushroom sauce. Great served over pasta.

Substitute caramelised onions for an onion sauce.

Add extra stock or milk for a thinner consistency.

Red Wine Sauce

This sauce is delicious served accompanying a steak, with sausages and mash or simply with grilled chicken. For a richer sauce substitute all the stock with wine.

Serves 4

2 onions, peeled and finely chopped

low calorie cooking spray

25g plain flour

225ml chicken/beef/vegetable stock

175ml red wine

salt and pepper

Fry the onions in the low calorie cooking spray until tender and golden brown, about 10 minutes. Don't rush this process otherwise the end result will be burnt bitter onions.

Stir in the flour, then gradually add the stock and wine, stirring continuously until there are no lumps. Simmer over a moderate heat until it thickens. Season to taste with a little salt and pepper.

Jayne's Tips

Omit the flour and simmer the sauce until it reduces in volume and thickens slightly.

Tomato and Garlic Sauce

If you're short on time to rustle up dinner then this recipe might just come in handy. It's absolutely delicious served over pasta, vegetables or couscous but could be used as a sauce for fish or chicken. If you have over-ripe tomatoes, then this is a perfect dish to use them up including any herbs you have lying around. Blitz the finished sauce if you prefer a less chunky sauce.

Serves 4

1 kg tomatoes

2 garlic cloves, peeled and chopped

2 teaspoons dried rosemary or
4 teaspoons of fresh, chopped

2 tablespoons balsamic vinegar

salt and pepper

Cut the tomatoes into chunks and place into a deep pan together with the garlic and rosemary. Cover the pan and cook over a low heat until the tomatoes have wilted down and created a sauce, stirring from time to time. Add the balsamic vinegar and season to taste with a little salt and pepper.

Jayne's Tips

If you don't want tomato skins in your sauce, remove them before making this recipe. To do this, cut a cross into their base and place them into a bowl. Cover with boiling water and leave for one minute, then transfer them to a bowl containing iced water. The skins should simply slip off. If not repeat the process.

Vanilla Cream

A fantastic alternative to whipped cream. Not only is it delicious but it's also very light in texture and really low in fat. So no excuses – there need never be a time when you can't have vanilla cream with your dessert!

Makes 750g

500g 0% Greek yoghurt/low fat fromage frais

250g Quark

vanilla extract (to taste)

sweetener (to taste)

Place the fromage frais and Quark into a mixing bowl adding enough vanilla extract and sweetener to taste. Blend together with a stick blender, wooden spoon or whisk until it's light and creamy, rather like whipped cream. Cover the bowl and refrigerate until required.

Jayne's Tips

Add the seeds from a vanilla pod, the zest of an orange or substitute almond extract instead of the vanilla (yummy with fresh peaches). Omit the Quark if you're not a fan, but the texture will be softer.

Vanilla Custard

A traditional vanilla custard is really delicious whether eaten hot or cold. If you want to omit the cornflour from the recipe do so but heat the custard over a really low heat to prevent the eggs from over cooking. I don't have much patience so using cornflour is always a safeguard for me.

Serves 4

500g skimmed milk

1 x vanilla pod (optional)
or 1 teaspoon vanilla extract

4 egg yolks

sweetener (to taste)

2 teaspoons cornflour

(Pictured on p.215 Apple and Blackberry Crumble)

Place the milk in a saucepan. Split the vanilla pod lengthways and with the end of a teaspoon, scrape down the pod removing all the vanilla seeds. Place these and the empty pod in the pan with the milk. If using vanilla extract add it to the milk. Bring the milk to the boil, cover, turn off the heat and leave to infuse for at least 20 minutes – longer if time allows. Remove the pod from the milk, reserving until later (see Jayne's Tips below).

In a jug or bowl mix together the egg yolks, sweetener, cornflour and a little of the infused milk. Transfer this mixture into the remaining infused milk. Bring to the boil over a low heat stirring continuously until the custard starts to thicken and coats the back of the spoon. The custard is now ready to serve.

Jayne's Tips

A small amount of cornflour prevents the eggs from over cooking and curdling. If you overheat your custard it will begin to resemble scrambled egg. Immediately place the saucepan in a bowl or sink of cold water and beat vigorously, you might just save it!

To prevent a skin from forming, place cling film directly onto the custard's surface.

Rinse the reserved empty vanilla pod under cold water, dry on kitchen paper, then add to a container of sugar or sweetener to make vanilla flavoured sugar.

Leftover egg whites can be placed into a lidded container and frozen until needed. Use to make a pavlova or roulade at a later date (see recipes on p.185 and p.187).

Desserts

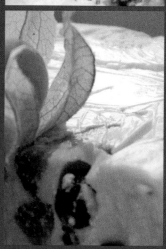

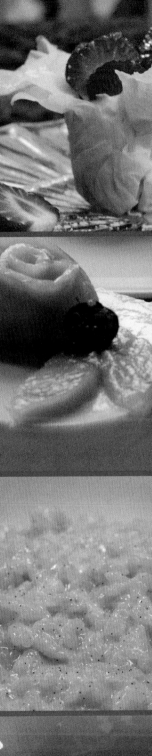

Fresh Fruit Pavlova

Pavlova is one of my favourite desserts. It's so light and fluffy, tastes divine and simply slips down. I've tried using sugar substitute when making the Pavlova base but feel it doesn't work here. However, pairing this with a lighter filling by using an alternative to cream creates, in my onion, an ideal compromise.

Serves 12

FOR THE MERINGUE

4 egg whites

300g caster sugar

2 teaspoons cornflour

1 teaspoon raspberry wine vinegar

1 teaspoon vanilla extract

FOR THE FILLING

1kg 0% Greek yoghurt or low fat fromage frais

500g Quark or fat free cream cheese

2 vanilla pods, split lengthways, seeds removed

2 teaspoons vanilla extract

sweetener (to taste) plus extra for dusting (optional)

seasonal fruit

fresh mint leaves to decorate (optional)

Preheat the oven to 140C/Gas 1.

Line a large baking tray with non-stick paper. On the underside of the paper draw a 25cm circle (I use a round tin as a template), this will form the area to be filled with the meringue. Turn over the paper so the ink side is against the tray.

Whisk the egg whites together until stiff then gradually beat in the sugar a little at a time until the mixture is thick and glossy.

Next, mix together the cornflour, raspberry wine vinegar and vanilla extract in a small bowl beating this into the meringue mixture. You should end up with a thick, stiff mixture holding its shape.

Spoon or pipe the meringue onto the paper and gently spread to fill the circle. Don't be too heavy handed here otherwise you'll knock out the air and end up with a biscuit.

Bake for 1 hour then reduce the temperature to 120C/Gas ¼ and bake for a further hour. Turn off the heat and cool completely inside the oven.

Once cold, remove the paper and place the meringue base onto a serving plate. Then make the filling.

For the filling mix together the yoghurt, Quark, vanilla seeds, vanilla extract and enough sweetener to taste. Spoon onto the meringue base and top with seasonal fruit. Dust with extra sweetener and decorate with fresh mint leaves.

Jayne's Tips

Add the filling to the meringue just before serving otherwise the meringue base will go soft. The base can be stored in an airtight container for several weeks. If it becomes soft, place on a baking tray and bake in a cool oven for about 30 minutes.

You could vary the flavour of the filling by substituting flavoured low fat hot chocolate powders, such as white chocolate for the vanilla seeds.

Raspberry Meringue Roulade

If you love fluffy marshmallows then you are going to enjoy this dessert. It's so light and soft. Just like the pavlova recipe, sugar substitute doesn't work here which is why sugar features in this recipe. But let's be realistic, one slice isn't going to put on weight. Eating half the roulade might though. However, it's not all calorie laden as the damage has been limited by substituting a cream filling with a lower calorie alternative.

Serves 12

low calorie cooking spray

4 egg whites

150g caster sugar

1 teaspoon cornflour

1 teaspoon raspberry wine vinegar

1 teaspoon vanilla extract

FOR THE FILLING

500g Quark or fat free cream cheese

2 teaspoons vanilla extract

zest 1 large orange, finely grated

sweetener (to taste)

seasonal fruit

Preheat the oven to 160C/Gas 3 and spray a 23cm x 32.5cm Swiss roll tin with the low calorie cooking spray. Line with non-stick paper, snipping the corners of the paper to fit and press down well so that the paper sticks to the tin.

Prepare the meringue by whisking the egg whites together until stiff. Gradually beat in the sugar until thick and glossy. Don't rush this process.

Mix together the cornflour, raspberry wine vinegar and vanilla extract in a small bowl, then whisk into the meringue. The meringue should become very stiff and hold its shape.

Spoon the meringue into the paper lined tin, levelling the surface with the back of the spoon. Don't press down too firmly to avoid pushing out the air. Bake in the oven until the meringue is a pale golden colour on top and feels slightly crisp and dry to the touch, about 20-25 minutes.

When cooked remove the tin from the oven and cover the surface with a sheet of non-stick baking paper. Place a cooling rack on top of the meringue and turn the tin and rack over so that the meringue is now resting on the papered rack. Remove the tin and peel off the paper. Leave to cool.

Prepare the filling by mixing together the Quark, vanilla extract, grated orange zest and enough sweetener to taste.

To assemble lift the non-stick paper, on which the meringue is placed, onto a large sheet of tin foil. Using a spatula carefully spread the filling over the surface of the meringue to within 1cm of the edges. Top with seasonal fruit. To form the roll, position the roulade with the longest length facing you, pick up the long edge of the paper and use it to gently roll up the meringue, pushing lightly away from you. You should end up with a Swiss roll shape. Tightly wrap in the paper and foil and transfer to the refrigerator keeping it wrapped until ready to serve.

Remove the foil and paper and transfer to a suitable serving plate. Cut into slices and serve with extra fresh fruit.

My Everyday Vanilla Cheesecake

Another one of my favourite desserts is cheesecake. I could eat it everyday, literally and still go back for more. Unfortunately, a traditional New York cheesecake is very high in fat, sugar and calories so it can only be eaten as a rare treat. Or so you may think. When I created this cheesecake I was ecstatic, I wanted to shout about it – seriously – little things make me so happy especially if they are dessert related. I even made a video – my first – and put it on YouTube because I was that excited. With my version you really can have your cake and eat it. Sorry it had to be said. This can be eaten everyday if you want to, without feeling guilty. It's a delicious alternative being low in fat, sugar and calories and using scan bran for the base gives you the added fibre too. It's equally delicious baked without the base.

Serves 12

FOR THE BASE

low calorie cooking spray

5 scan bran, roughly crushed (available from Health Food shops)

30g cocoa

2 eggs

sweetener (to taste)

FOR THE FILLING

1.5kg Quark or fat free cream cheese

4 teaspoons of vanilla extract

1 vanilla pod, split lengthways, seeds removed

sweetener (to taste)

60g plain flour

350g fat free vanilla yoghurt

3 eggs

FOR THE TOPPING

175g fat free vanilla yoghurt

seasonal fruit

FOR THE FRUIT COULIS

soft berry fruits

sweetener

lemon juice

Preheat the oven to 180C/Gas 4 and spray a 23cm loose-bottomed tin with the low calorie cooking spray.

To make the base, put the crushed scan bran into a bowl pouring over enough boiling water to soak slightly. Mix to form a rough paste then stir in the cocoa, eggs and sweetener to taste. Pour the mixture into the tin, spreading to completely cover the base. Bake for 15 minutes, then leave to cool. Increase the oven temperature to 220C/Gas 7.

Mix the filling ingredients together until smooth, either by hand or with a mixer. Pour this mixture over the baked base, smoothing the surface with a spatula. Bake for 10 minutes, then reduce the heat to 110C/ Gas ¼ and bake for a further 25 minutes.

Turn off the oven and wedge a wooden spoon between the door and the oven to keep it ajar. This allows the cheesecake to cool slowly, preventing the surface from cracking. Cool inside for 2 hours.

Remove the cooled cheesecake from the oven and pour the remaining yoghurt over the top. Cover with cling film and chill, preferably overnight. Serve with seasonal fruit.

For an impressive dessert, serve drizzled with a fruit coulis. Blend together any fruit in season; strawberries are great, using a food processor or stick blender. Add sweetener to taste and a squeeze of lemon juice. (Taste as you go to get the balance right). For a smooth coulis pass through a sieve using a wooden spoon or ladle, although you will be discarding valuable fibre. Chill until required.

White Chocolate and Strawberry Cheesecake

Chocolate, strawberries, cheesecake - a marriage made in heaven and who would've thought you could indulge in these guilty pleasures! This is a wonderful and impressive dessert for a dinner party or special occasion. Don't let on that it's a lighter version, as no one will ever know the difference, leaving you to bask in the compliments. Plus, you can sit back knowing that you're in control and watching your weight with every delicious spoonful.

Serves 12

FOR THE BASE

low calorie cooking spray

8 digestive biscuits, crushed

1 egg white

FOR THE FILLING

12 sheets gelatine (vegetarian alternative or powder equivalent, prepared according to packet instructions)

1.5kg Quark or fat free cream cheese

4 teaspoons of vanilla extract

1 vanilla pod, split lengthways, seeds removed

sweetener (to taste)

6 x 11g sachets low fat white chocolate flavour powder

500g 0% Greek yoghurt or low fat fromage frais

500g strawberries, ideally the same height, stalks removed, halved lengthways

Preheat the oven to 180C/Gas 4 and spray the base of a 23cm loose-bottomed tin with the low calorie cooking spray.

For the base, mix the crushed biscuits with the egg white. Then with the back of a spoon, or you can use wet fingers, press this mixture into the base of the tin making sure it is covered. Bake for 10 minutes then leave to cool.

Separate the gelatine sheets and place them into a bowl containing cold water. Leave until completely softened, about 2-3 minutes. When soft, squeeze out the excess water and place the softened gelatine into a bowl with 3 tablespoons of water. Microwave until completely dissolved, about 30-40 seconds. Put aside to cool.

Place the Quark, vanilla extract, vanilla seeds, sweetener, chocolate powder and yoghurt in a food processor and process until smooth, scraping down the sides of the bowl every now and again. Add the cooled gelatine and mix again until everything is combined.

To assemble, line the tin with cling film (see Jayne's Tips below) and pour a little of the cheesecake mixture over the biscuit base to a depth of about 5mm. Press a strawberry half, cut-side against the side of the cling film/tin, resting the bottom of the strawberry onto the mixture.

FOR THE TOPPING

250g 0% Greek yoghurt

1 x 11g sachet low fat white chocolate flavour powder

Repeat this process until you have formed a complete ring of strawberries around the inside of the tin. Chop any remaining strawberries, including any scraps and mix into the cheesecake mixture. Pour this into the tin smoothing over the surface. Refrigerate until set, about 2 hours.

When set, make the topping by mixing together the yoghurt and hot chocolate powder and pour this over the top, smoothing to level. Cover and chill again, preferably overnight.

To serve, if not using cling film, very carefully run a palette knife between the tin and the edge of the cheesecake to loosen the sides, then unclip the tin and remove. If using cling film just peel away once the tin has been unclipped.

Serve topped with seasonal soft fruit and a fruit coulis (see recipe on p.191).

Jayne's Tips

Substitute the white chocolate powder with other flavours to make a variety of different flavours.

A strip of cling film or acetate lined around the inside of the tin makes unmoulding easier and produces a neater finish.

Substitute the Quark for very low fat cottage cheese. If using cottage cheese blend in a food processor for a smooth texture.

The halved strawberries, around the outside of the cheesecake, are purely for presentation purposes only. You can omit this stage by chopping all the strawberries, adding them to the cheesecake filling and pouring this into the tin.

Always Time for Rice Pudding

We all need a dessert from time to time that will fill that hole but won't blow the waistline. This dessert does it for me. I personally like it with a little sweetener and an extra drizzle of milk. It reminds me of my childhood. Substitute the drizzle of milk for fat free Greek yoghurt or a drizzle of low fat cream. My daughter loves hers with a good dollop of strawberry jam in the centre, and my grand daughter prefers hers mixed with chocolate spread. My mother always baked her pudding in the oven, which felt an eternity to wait for when you're a young child - actually equally as long as a grown-up too. This recipe is really quick so no excuses, there's always time for rice pudding. Any leftovers can be eaten cold – equally delicious or reheated in the microwave until piping hot.

Serves 6

150g short grain rice

1 litre skimmed milk

1 teaspoon vanilla extract

1 vanilla pod (optional) split length-ways, seeds removed

sweetener (to taste)

Place all the ingredients, except sweetener, into a pan. Bring to a boil, cover with a lid and reduce the heat to low. Cook, stirring occasionally, until the rice is tender and the milk is absorbed, about 25-30 minutes. Keep an eye on the pan to avoid the milk from boiling over.

Add sweetener to taste and serve or if you like your pudding a bit thicker leave covered off the heat for another 10-15 minutes. Reheat if necessary and serve with whatever accompaniment that tickles your fancy.

BRULEED RICE PUDDING

Prepare as above and spoon into individual dishes. Leave to cool. (This option is also useful if you have any leftover rice pudding).

Just before serving sprinkle the surface with caster sugar and place under a hot grill until the sugar has melted and turned golden brown. A blowtorch is also excellent for this job if you have one. (Make sure your husband isn't looking though!)

Jayne's Tips

Caramelised sweetener simply doesn't work and tastes and smells awful so stick to a little caster sugar for the bruleed version.

I find the easiest way to remove the seeds from a halved vanilla pod is to use the end of a teaspoon - it never fails to do the job.

Chocolate Rice Pudding

If there are times when you crave something sweet and chocolatey, or you're a chocoholic and find it hard to stop eating once you start, this dessert might just fit the bill. Not only does it give you that chocolate kick, it's extremely filling too. So say goodbye to the temptation of demolishing a whole box of chocolates in one sitting!

Be warned, once your family have sampled this you'll be forever supplying it in vast quantities. I love this served with one cube of chocolate swirled in just before serving – simply luxurious and decadent or substitute the chocolate cube with a low fat hot chocolate powder - there are endless flavours available.

Serves 4

1 quantity of basic rice pudding (see recipe on p.195)

4 cubes of chocolate or 2 sachets low fat chocolate flavour powder

Prepare and cook the basic rice pudding (see previous recipe). Then, if using the chocolate powder, stir into the rice pudding. If you're going down the decadent route, divide the pudding between bowls (if sharing!) and place 1 chocolate cube into the centre of each bowl. All you need do is stand back and watch it gently form a puddle of melted chocolate.

If you want to eat this hot do so now. Personally I can't wait and have to eat it straight away. If you prefer to eat it cold, or have any leftovers, simply chill in the refrigerator until required. Serve dolloped with vanilla cream (see recipe on p.181) for that extra creamy touch.

Jayne's Tips

Add the grated zest of an orange for that extra zingy taste.

Any Day Summer Pudding

I was never one to go overboard on the traditional Summer Pudding, made with stale bread. My version is made with sponge fingers, a lot nicer in my opinion. Made with any soft fruit in season, it's a good standby year round as a quick and delicious dessert!

Serves 6

250g Quark or fat free cream cheese

360g low fat fromage frais

1 vanilla pod, split lengthways, seeds removed

1 teaspoon vanilla extract

sweetener (to taste)

150ml sugar free lemon and elderflower, slightly sparkling water

13 sponge fingers (depending on size of basin)

420g mixed berries (or fruits in season)

Prepare a 1 litre pudding basin by lining it with cling film, leaving enough cling film overhanging at the top. This will be used later to cover the surface.

Mix together the Quark, fromage frais, vanilla seeds, vanilla extract and sweetener until combined. Then, pour the sparkling water into a shallow dish and working with one sponge finger at a time, dunk into the water so that it starts to absorb some of the liquid. Don't saturate the sponge fingers, as they will disintegrate. Place the sponge finger, sugar side against the cling film, vertically around the inside of the basin. Repeat with the remaining fingers to line the dish.

Once lined, spread a little of the filling over the base of the dish. This will create the top (when the pudding is turned out). Layer the basin with the fruit and filling, ending with a layer of the filling. Next, take a sharp knife and cut off any sponge fingers that poke out over the top of the basin. Smooth over the surface to level. (This will become the bottom). Lift up the overhanging cling film and use to cover the surface. Refrigerate for at least 4 hours, or preferably overnight.

To unmould, fold back the cling film and place a serving plate over the top. Quickly turn the basin and plate over so that the plate is now on the bottom. What should happen (fingers crossed) is that the Summer Pudding should slip free from the basin and drop onto the plate. Carefully lift off the basin and gently remove the cling film exposing your gorgeous summer dessert.

Serve on it's own or drizzled with pouring yoghurt and extra fruit.

Jayne's Tips

Use a packet of frozen mixed berries (thawed) during winter or when soft fruit is expensive.

Tiramisu

Tiramisu literally means "pick me up". If traditionally prepared it's not only delicious but extremely rich, laden with many calories. I know a little of what you fancy does you good - or so the saying goes - but honestly once you taste a traditionally made, good Tiramisu you are left wanting more, especially if you have a sweet tooth! However, there will be no need to "pick you up" after eating this version as it's made light in fat and short on the calories so you could indulge in this delectable delight whenever you fancy a treat without the guilt! Use sugar free coffee syrup if you can find it or alternatively double up on the coffee. For a special dessert use coffee liqueur instead of the sugar free coffee syrup, but beware of the extra calories. If serving for children use orange zest and juice in the filling instead of the coffee syrup. This dessert can be made and served in an attractive glass bowl or individual glasses for an impressive finish to a wonderful meal.

Serves 6-8

150ml strong black coffee, preferably filtered

150ml sugar free coffee syrup (optional)

FOR THE FILLING

500g Quark or fat free cream cheese

500g low fat fromage frais

sweetener (to taste)

1 vanilla pod, split lengthways, seeds removed

1 teaspoon vanilla extract

16 sponge finger biscuits

FOR THE TOPPING

1 x 11g sachet low fat chocolate flavour powder

Firstly mix the coffee with the sugar free coffee syrup in a shallow dish.

In a large bowl prepare the filling by mixing the Quark, low fat fromage frais, sweetener, vanilla seeds and vanilla extract until combined.

Take 8 sponge finger biscuits and dunk them into the coffee mixture until they start to soften. Transfer the fingers to the serving dish forming a layer on the bottom then spread half the filling over the top. Repeat with the remaining sponge fingers, discarding any excess liquid. Spoon over the last of the filling smoothing over the surface. Lastly, sprinkle over the chocolate powder and cover the dish with cling film. Refrigerate for at least 3 hours to allow the flavours to develop.

Jayne's Tips

Find something to do for three hours and then dive in and enjoy!

Summers Here Strawberry Tarts

I just love strawberry tart. It conjures up memories of the summer. But who wants to wait for the sun to shine? These delicious little tarts are not only light to eat but are light on the waistline too, so you can't go wrong. They're wonderful for a teatime treat, summer dessert or part of a picnic. I find that there's always a healthier alternative to high calorie and fatty foods and here is my alternative to the strawberry tart. Swap the strawberries for any other fruit in season. Make them individually or one large one for a stunning centrepiece.

Serves 4

4 sheets filo pastry

low calorie cooking spray

sweetener (to taste)

240g low fat fromage frais

130g Quark or fat free cream cheese

1 vanilla pod, split lengthways,
seeds removed (optional)

1 teaspoon vanilla extract

fresh strawberries

Preheat your oven to 180C/Gas 4.

Firstly prepare the filo tarts by taking one piece of the filo pastry and cutting it into four equal sized pieces (make sure you cover the other three sheets with a damp tea towel so that they don't dry out). Spray all four pieces with the low calorie cooking spray then sprinkle over a little sweetener. Place the pastry pieces on top of each other to form a star shape that will form your pastry case. Be careful at this point as the pastry case is quite delicate and can easily tear. Carefully pick up the pastry and ease gently into the mould to line the sides and base. Repeat with the remaining pastry sheets. Place the filled mould onto a baking tray and then bake in the oven until crisp and golden brown, about 15 minutes. Remove the mould from the oven and leave to go cold. Store the pastry cases in an airtight container until ready to fill.

Make the filling by mixing together the fromage frais, Quark, vanilla seeds, vanilla extract and a little sweetener. Spoon into the pastry cases and top with sliced strawberries. Sprinkle with a dusting of sweetener and serve immediately.

Jayne's Tips

Fill the pastry cases just before serving to avoid the pastry cases going soggy.

A large muffin tin is great but use whatever tin you have available.

If the stored pastry cases become soft, warm them in a gentle oven until firm, then cool before filling.

Thai Rice Cake

A rice cake, don't they only come in packets? Well actually no they don't! This rice cake makes a delicious and unusual dessert that has a lovely soft texture with the hint of an Asian flavour. If you're a carb fan like me, you're going to love it! As the cake cools a little liquid might seep out, which is completely normal and a result of using low fat/sugar products. Simply pour off the excess liquid or mop up with some kitchen paper. Make the day before to allow it to cool before decorating, it will be worth the wait!

Serves 12

low fat cooking spray

250g Thai or jasmine rice

9 cardamom pods, seeds crushed and husks discarded

2 bay leaves

1 litre Koko coconut milk

sweetener (to taste)

300g 0% Greek yoghurt or low fat fromage frais

6 eggs, separated

FOR THE TOPPING

500g 0% Greek yoghurt or low fat fromage frais

250g Quark or fat free cream cheese

sweetener (to taste)

1 teaspoon vanilla extract

zest 1 lime, finely grated

fresh mixed berries to decorate

Preheat the oven to 180C/Gas 4. Spray a 23cm loose-bottomed tin with the low calorie cooking spray. Line the base with a non-stick paper disk and place onto a baking sheet. Put the rice in a saucepan, cover with water and bring to the boil. Continue to boil for 3 minutes, drain the rice in a sieve and return the rice back to the pan with the crushed cardamom pods, bay leaves and Koko milk. Bring to the boil and simmer for 20 minutes, stirring occasionally. Then switch off the heat and leave to cool.

Remove the bay leaves from the mixture and tip the rice into a bowl. Stir in the sweetener, fromage frais and egg yolks. Then whisk the egg whites in a bowl until stiff and fold them into the rice. Pour the mixture into the lined cake tin, leveling the surface with a palette knife.

Bake until the cake has risen and is golden brown, about 40-45 minutes. (Don't worry it will sink slightly upon cooling). Once cooled, leave the cake in its tin, cover and refrigerate overnight.

For the topping beat together the ingredients until smooth. Remove the cake from its tin by running a palette knife between the cake and the tin. Place a serving plate on top and quickly turn the plate and tin upside down so that the top of the cake is now on the plate. Remove the tin and the non-stick paper disk; this is now the top of your cake. Spread the topping over the cake in a swirling motion, being gentle as the cake will be very soft. Decorate with fresh mixed berries.

Keep refrigerated until required dusting with a little sweetener just before serving.

Fruit Creams

There are times when a pot of yoghurt just doesn't cut it! I love yoghurt but sometimes you need something to sink your teeth into and these little pots will do the trick. They are quick and easy to make and the family will love them. Great for a light summer dessert.

These creams can be set in one large mould or into individual cocktail or wine glasses for a special presentation to make a stunning dessert.

For each cream pot you will need

150ml fat free yoghurt, any flavour

sweetener (to taste)

1 sheet gelatine or vegetarian alternative

2 teaspoons water

seasonal fruit to decorate (optional)

Mix the yoghurt with the sweetener and set to one side. Place the sheet of gelatine into a small bowl containing cold water, leave to soften for a few minutes. Then squeeze out the water and place the softened gelatine in a microwaveable bowl with 2 teaspoons of water. Heat for 30 seconds. Cool for 2 minutes then stir into the yoghurt. Pour into the mould (see Jayne's Tips below), smoothing over the top. Refrigerate for at least 2 hours or until set.

To serve, remove the cling film from the mould and place the mould onto a dessert plate. Run a thin knife around the inside and carefully lift off the mould - the cream should slide through and be left behind on the plate. If a little stubborn a gentle shake should do the trick. Decorate with seasonal fruit and wait for the compliments.

Jayne's Tips

Layer the creams with fresh fruit, or make two different flavoured creams and layer them in a glass to add visual impact to your deliciously tasting, creamy treat.

There is no need to buy specialist moulds - use small empty baked bean cans. Remove the bottom from each can so you have a ring. Place a piece of cling film on the work surface and put the ring on top. Pick up the edges of the cling film and wrap around the outside of the can - you should end up with a ring mould with a cling film bottom. Set the moulds onto a tray or plate that will fit easily into the refrigerator.

Sparkling Berry Jellies

If you like having something sweet and refreshing at the end of a meal, these wonderful jellies are just the ticket and best of all won't blow your waistline as they're so light, perfect after a heavy meal or an after school summertime treat. Don't try setting a jelly with fresh pineapple or kiwi fruit as they both contain an enzyme that will prevent a jelly setting.

Jellies can be set in almost anything. Individual moulds, one large family mould or terrine, tea-cups or in decorative wine glasses for an elegant dessert – endless ways for any occasion. The jellies are best prepared the day before as it can be time consuming setting each layer, although the end product is really worth the effort.

Makes enough to fill 3 x 300ml wine glasses

4 sheets of gelatine

50ml water

sweetener (to taste)

568ml lemon and elderflower slightly sparkling sugar free water

seasonal fruit

Fill a bowl with cold water. Drop the separated gelatine sheets into the water, submerging under the water. Leave until completely softened, about 5 minutes. Remove the softened gelatine from the water, gently squeezing to remove any excess water. Place them into a small bowl, adding 50ml of water. Microwave until completely dissolved, about 40 seconds. (The gelatine can also be dissolved in a small saucepan over a very low heat. The liquid should look clear once dissolved). Then stir in a little sweetener and leave until cool, about 5 minutes. Stir this liquid into the sparkling water.

Start layering the jellies by placing a small amount of fruit into the bottom of each glass. Pour in enough jelly so that it just covers the fruit. Place the glasses in the fridge to set - this can take up to an hour. Repeat the layers until the glasses are full. Refrigerate the jellies until completely set.

Serve on their own, with seasonal fruit or with a lovely dollop of vanilla cream (see recipe on p.181).

Jayne's Tips

If time is limited or you're not particularly fussy about having your jelly layered, simply tumble the fruit into your chosen glasses followed by the liquid jelly. Then refrigerate until set. As the jellies set the fruit will rise to the surface leaving some fruitless jelly at the bottom - equally delicious but not as attractive.

You could substitute sugar free lemonade instead of sparkling water, which was a hit with my kids.

Strawberry Ice Cream

Surprisingly I am not a huge fan of ice cream, I can take it or leave it, but I know there are many of you who just adore it, my daughter included, who claims to be the Ice Cream Queen! If you simply love the stuff then this might just be what you've been waiting for. Its claim to fame is that you can eat this version without any guilt because the calorific content has been reduced dramatically.

Alter the flavour using any type of flavoured yoghurt, adding fresh fruit or even low fat hot chocolate powders. Have a go and experiment.

A note on ice cream machines, they don't cost the earth. The more affordable models require you to freeze the ice cream bowl overnight so take this into account before purchasing. Many years ago I purchased an electric version that has an in-built chilling compartment, but these tend to be larger machines requiring more storage space and are more expensive, but I haven't looked back. The good news is that this recipe is also easy to prepare without a machine.

Makes 1 pint

450g fat free strawberry yoghurt

sweetener (to taste)

125g Quark or fat free cream cheese

Mix all the ingredients together in a large jug, which will be ideal for pouring the liquid ice cream into the machine. Experience will later tell you if your taste buds require more sweetener added at this stage. Pour the liquid into the machine and churn until a firm 'ice cream' consistency has been reached.

If preparing by hand, pour the liquid into a plastic container, cover and freeze until the sides are almost firm, between 30-60 minutes. Remove from the freezer, tip into a chilled bowl and beat with an electric whisk and re-freeze. Repeat this process at least twice more, up to a maximum of five times, in order to break up the ice crystals so that a smooth consistency is obtained upon freezing.

Serve by itself, accompanying any dessert or with fresh seasonal fruit. But then who am I to tell you how to eat ice cream!

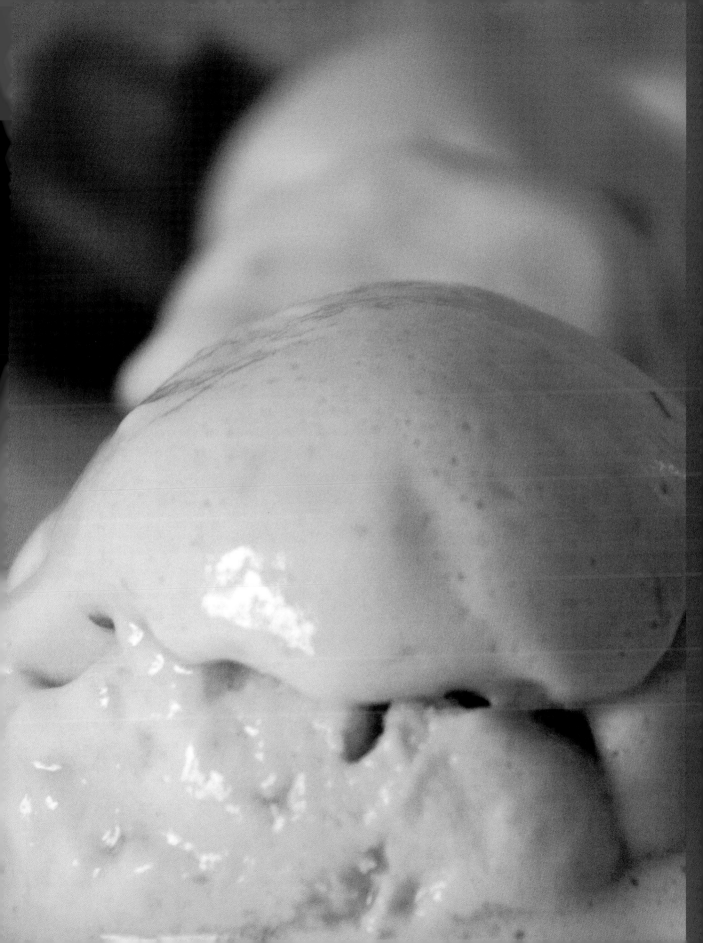

White Chocolate Pots

If you love chocolate and just want something small and indulgent then try this. Lovely as an elegant dessert cooked in small ovenproof coffee cups and served on a saucer with a teaspoon.

Makes 4-6 depending on size of cups/moulds

500ml skimmed milk

1 vanilla pod, split lengthways, seeds removed

6 x 11g sachets low fat white chocolate flavour powder

2 egg yolks

2 whole eggs

sweetener (to taste)

fresh fruit to serve (optional)

Preheat the oven to 140C/Gas 1. Line the base of a deep baking tin with kitchen paper and set aside.

Place the milk in a saucepan with the split vanilla pod and reserved seeds. Stir in the chocolate powder and heat until hot but not boiling. Whisk together the egg yolks, whole eggs and sweetener in a medium bowl. Remove the milk from the heat and add one-third to the eggs stirring well. Stir in the remaining milk then strain through a sieve into a jug.

Pour the custard into the cups and place the cups into the tin. Pour in enough hot water so that it reaches half way up the sides of the cups (the water prevents the custards from over cooking). Bake until the centre of the custards are just firm when pressed with your finger, about 20-30 minutes. Cover the top of the custards with a sheet of non-stick baking paper if they begin to brown.

When cooked, remove the cups from the water, leave to cool thoroughly then chill in the refrigerator for at least 1 hour. Serve decorated with fresh fruit.

Jayne's Tips

For variety substitute the white chocolate flavour powder
with other chocolate flavours.

You may also find it easier to pour the water into the tin
when it's on the oven shelf.

Decorate with chocolate buttons, sugared violets or a
strawberry drizzled with chocolate.

Apple and Blackberry Crumble

Another one of my favourite desserts is crumble. I just love the crunchy topping. Unfortunately that delicious topping contains fat, sugar and flour along with eye watering amounts of calories making it one of those 'should I, shouldn't I decisions'. This recipe comes in at a very close second in terms of crunchiness and flavour. It also means that it can be eaten a little more regularly than an original crumble as it contains healthy porridge oats! Just try it and see. What do you have to lose?

Serves 4

FOR THE FILLING

400g apples, peeled weight

1 vanilla pod, split lengthways, seeds removed (optional)

400g blackberries

sweetener (to taste)

FOR THE CRUMBLE TOPPING

3 tablespoons golden syrup

150g porridge oats

Core and slice the apples and place them with the vanilla pod and seeds in a saucepan with 2 tablespoons of water. Cover and cook gently until softened, then sweeten to taste.

Pour the blackberries into an ovenproof dish, sprinkle with a little sweetener and top with the apples, discarding the vanilla pod.

Next make the crumble. The easiest way to measure golden syrup is to dip a tablespoon into boiling water, then immediately dip the spoon into the syrup, scooping up a level spoonful (this makes the syrup simply slip off). Pour the syrup into a medium sized bowl and microwave until runny, about 30 seconds. Add the porridge oats, mixing well, so that the syrup coats the oats. Sprinkle this over the surface of the fruit.

Place the filled dish onto a baking tray and bake until bubbling and the top is crunchy and golden, about 25-30 minutes. Leave to rest for 5 minutes or so and then serve with vanilla custard, cream or ice cream (see recipes on p.182, p.181 and p.211). Divine!

Index